Light and Delicious Cookbook

by Karen Taggart

Ideals Publishing Corporation • Nashville, Tennessee 37214

CONTENTS

INTRODUCTION 4

BREADS, CAKES & COOKIES 11

PIES & FRUIT DESSERTS 20

PUDDINGS & CUSTARDS 29

SHERBETS & ICES 34

TOPPINGS & SAUCES 38

BREAKFAST SPECIALTIES 44

MAIN DISHES 49

VEGETARIAN DISHES 59

SALADS 63

INDEX 64

First published as *No Sugar Cooking*
ISBN 0-8249-3076-2
Copyright © MCMLXXXV by Ideals Publishing Corp.
All rights reserved.
Printed and bound in the United States of America.

Published by Ideals Publishing Corporation
Nelson Place at Elm Hill Pike
P.O. Box 148000
Nashville, Tennessee 37214-8000

Cover Photo:
Hawaiian Meatballs, 52

Low-Cal Vegetable Dip with
assorted fresh vegetables, page 60

INTRODUCTION

The *Light and Delicious Cookbook* was written for everyone who wants to cut down on sugar—the frustrated dieter, the diabetic, anyone concerned with fitness, well-being, and a sound dietary program. The bases for my recipes are the Diabetic Exchange Guide, enhanced by my own creations, and a love of cooking (and eating) that began when I was young.

For as long as I can remember, I have enjoyed cooking—particularly sweets like chocolate cake, raisin cookies, and apple pie. As a child, my "perfect" day was one when *my* chore was to prepare dinner, instead of doing other household tasks. My cooking skills were well-nurtured, and they grew into a love for the gourmet.

When I got married, my husband, a physician, declared that when he got fat, I could get fat—in that order. That sounded all right to me at the time, especially since I didn't plan to gain weight anyway. I found, however, that it wasn't easy cooking the foods I enjoy and keeping my weight under control, too. Hence, I started what became an all-too-familiar pattern: whenever I put on a few extra pounds, I became frustrated and tried a new diet. I must have tried virtually every new diet that hit the market. With each new diet, my husband would say, "If you really want to lose weight, you should follow the Diabetic Exchange Guide." When I finally heeded his advice, I discovered he was right. I lost weight, and the menus I planned did not lose the variety I enjoy.

Although I know I can shed pounds with the Diabetic Exchange Diet, my love of sweets has never allowed me to adopt it as a full-time guide. Still, I am concerned about sugar consumption for reasons other than my weight. The incidence of diabetes in my family's medical history is high. I often fear that I might contract the disease, and I know from experience the problems it causes. One of my grandfathers, an uncle, and two cousins all were diabetics. In fact, one of those cousins died in his teens because he couldn't stick to his diet. I remember how frustrated my grandfather was going without the desserts that he loved. My grandmother used to lock her dipping chocolate in a cedar chest so my grandfather wouldn't have so much trouble leaving such things alone. My grandfather would have loved my Rich Chocolate Cake with Banana

Freeze or my Chocolate Coconut Cake with Cherry Topping.

Fear and empathy prompted me to convert and create recipes with the diabetic in mind. Hoping to create recipes low in sugar, yet satisfying to the sweet tooth, I developed new versions of traditional desserts, such as, Carrot Cake, Rice Pudding, and Company Fresh Peach Pie, versions that are dense in nutrients and safe for diabetics.

In creating my No Sugar recipes, I've tried to make sure that the serving sizes are large enough to satisfy a big appetite. I firmly believe that the only diet that works is one that supplies plenty of good food. My Clam Chowder or Vegetarian Spaghetti hardly leaves room for a diet-destroying dessert—unless, of course, it's one that I designed especially for this book. (Keep in mind that many of my dessert recipes were not created to be meal supplements; many were intended to replace the breakfast meal.) For small appetites, my recipes are a real bonus. Many of the servings can easily be cut in half to reduce the already low calorie count even more.

Big appetite or small, dieter or diabetic, a feast of wonderful foods is contained in these pages. My mouth waters as I thumb through the recipes and remember the flavors of my favorite dishes. Tamale Cheese Pie, Chicken and Broccoli Casserole, and Tuna Cabbage Dinner are but a few of the delights that urge me back to my kitchen. I hope you will join me.

SPECIAL INGREDIENTS FOR NO SUGAR COOKING

Because of the special nature of these recipes, some of the ingredients might be unfamiliar to you. The following paragraphs discuss those ingredients.

Artificial Sweeteners

To enhance my dessert recipes, I rely heavily on artificial sweeteners. The different brands of sweeteners vary greatly in flavor, quality, and price. To find one acceptable to you, test the brands available in your area.

The finest sugar substitute I have found is aspartame, popularly known as NutraSweet. It usually appears under the trade name Equal. Unfortunately, NutraSweet does have a limitation: it cannot sustain long periods of heat. I can use

NutraSweet in my stove-top recipes simply by adding the sweetener just before the end of the cooking time. In recipes that require baking, however, I use a sweetener that is not sensitive to heat.

All recipes that require a sweetener direct you to use an amount equal to a given amount of sugar. Since each brand of sweetener has its own conversion ratio, you must follow the manufacturer's directions carefully. Remember that the level of sweetness can be changed. If you normally do not care for sweet desserts, you may want to lessen the amount of sweetener for a particular recipe. Also, for recipes that specify a *brown* sugar substitute, you may use a regular artificial sweetener, if you prefer it.

Natural Butter-flavored Granules

These granules are sold under the trade name Butter Buds. For recipes that require *liquid* butter-flavored granules, prepare the buds as the package directs. Recipes that call for just the dry granules require no preparation at all.

Imitation Salad Dressing

When shopping for this ingredient, remember that imitation salad dressing is generally lower in calories than imitation mayonnaise. Since the calorie count varies from one brand to the next, read the ingredient label to be sure that the brand you choose is as low in calories as you desire. When water is listed on the label before oil, the product will have fewer calories than one listing oil first.

Water-packed Tuna

Recipes that call for tuna indicate *water-packed* tuna because of its low calorie level. If water-packed tuna is not available, use oil-packed tuna that has been drained and rinsed.

THE DIABETIC EXCHANGE GUIDE

The Diabetic Exchange Guide breaks down a diabetic's daily nutritional requirements into six food groups. Each group contains a list of individual food items and portion sizes that the diabetic is allowed to eat. (These lists appear on pages 6 through 9.) Within each list, the individual is free to substitute one item for another as long as the portion sizes are observed. The Diabetic Exchanges are *the* guide to balanced, low-calorie, nutritionally dense meals, the basis of any sound diet or nutrition plan.

The Exchange lists presented in this book are based on the *Exchange Lists for Meal Planning*, prepared by Committees of the American Diabetes Association, Inc. and The American Dietetic Association, in cooperation with the National Institute of Arthritis, Metabolism and Digestive Diseases, the National Heart and Lung Institute, the National Institute of Health, the Public Health Service, and the United States Department of Health, Education and Welfare.

The Bonus Group

To assist in menu planning, Exchange Guides are listed with each of my recipes. To the usual six groups I have added a seventh, the Bonus Group, not ordinarily found in the Diabetic Exchange Guide. In the amounts allotted, foods in the Bonus Group are relatively low in calories, and they are the key to the special character of my cookbook. They can add the extra, palate-pleasing zip that a diabetic's or calorie-counter's diet often lacks. Bonus foods included in a given recipe are underlined in the list of ingredients for easy identification. The Exchange Guide that follows each recipe indicates the number of Bonus foods (Extras) present in that recipe.

The Bonus Group has two subgroups. The first one includes the following foods in the stated amounts. These foods register approximately 50 calories each per serving; one serving from this subgroup is allowed daily.

clam juice	1 cup
tomato juice	1 cup
tomato paste	¼ cup
tomato puree	½ cup
tomato sauce (no sugar added)	½ cup
vegetable juice	1 cup

Note: This subgroup also includes commercially prepared diet products that contain less than 40 calories per serving.

The second Bonus subgroup contains foods that register approximately 10 calories each per serving. Up to three selections from this subgroup are allowed daily. These foods include:

barbecue, chili, or steak sauce	2 level teaspoons
caraway, poppy, sesame, or sunflower seeds	1 level teaspoon
cocoa or carob	1 level teaspoon
coconut, shredded	1 level teaspoon
cornstarch or flour	1 level teaspoon
Parmesan or Romano cheese, grated	1 level teaspoon

A total of four Bonus foods is allowed daily. These bonuses could increase your calorie intake by about 85, if all four are included, but the count is low enough to make a delightful difference in a diabetic's menu and should be of little concern to the weight-conscious dieter. It is a known fact that minor slips of 40 to 50 calories per day are relatively insignificant to diabetics or to overweight dieters. Furthermore, the diabetic who is not overweight does not have to count calories, so the few extra calories provided by these foods should not be alarming.

DIABETIC EXCHANGE LISTS

Vegetable Exchanges
One exchange of vegetables contains about 5 grams of carbohydrate, 2 grams of protein, and 25 calories. One exchange equals ½ cup.

Asparagus	Mushrooms
Bean sprouts	Okra
Beets	Onions
Broccoli	Rhubarb
Brussels sprouts	Rutabaga
Cabbage	Sauerkraut
Carrots	String beans,
Cauliflower	green or yellow
Celery	Summer squash
Eggplant	Tomatoes
Green pepper	Tomato juice
Greens:	Turnips
Beet	Vegetable juice
Chard	cocktail
Collard	Zucchini
Dandelion	
Kale	
Mustard	
Spinach	
Turnip	

One exchange equals ½ cup if only one serving is eaten per day (otherwise, ½ cup serving equals 1 bread exchange).

Jerusalem artichokes	Winter squash,
Peas, green	(acorn or
Pumpkin	butternut)

One exchange equals unlimited amount if eaten raw.

Chicory	Lettuce
Chinese cabbage	Parsley
Cucumbers	Pickles, dill
Endive	Radishes
Escarole	Watercress

Note: Starchy vegetables are found in the Bread Exchanges.

Milk Exchanges
One exchange of milk contains 12 grams of carbohydrate, 8 grams of protein, a trace of fat, and 80 calories. Each portion equals 1 exchange.

Non-Fat Fortified Milk:

Skim or non-fat milk	1 cup
Powdered (non-fat dry milk)	⅓ cup
Canned, evaporated skim milk	½ cup
Buttermilk made with skim milk	1 cup
Yogurt made with skim milk, plain, unflavored	1 cup

Low-Fat Fortified Milk:

1% fat fortified milk (add ½ fat exchange)	1 cup
2% fat fortified milk (add 1 fat exchange)	1 cup
Yogurt made with 2% fortified milk, plain, unflavored (add 1 fat exchange)	1 cup

Whole Milk (add 2 fat exchanges):

Whole Milk	1 cup
Canned, evaporated whole milk	½ cup
Buttermilk made with whole milk	1 cup
Yogurt made with whole milk, plain, unflavored	1 cup

Fruit Exchanges
One exchange of fruit contains 10 grams of carbohydrate and 40 calories. Each portion equals 1 exchange.

Apple	1 small
Apple juice	⅓ cup
Applesauce, unsweetened	½ cup
Apricots, fresh	2 medium
Apricots, dried	4 halves
Banana	½ small
Berries:	
Blackberries	½ cup
Blueberries	½ cup
Loganberries	½ cup
Raspberries	½ cup
Strawberries	¾ cup
Cherries	10 large
Cider	⅓ cup
Cranberries	(see note)
Dates	2
Figs, fresh	1
Figs, dried	1
Fruit cocktail, unsweetened	½ cup
Grapefruit	½
Grapefruit juice	½ cup
Grapefruit sections	½ cup
Grapes	12
Grape juice	¼ cup

Assorted Fruit Ices, page 34

Kiwi	1 medium
Mango	½ small
Melons:	
Cantaloupe	¼ small
Honeydew	⅛ medium
Watermelon	1 cup
Nectarine	1 small
Orange	1 small
Orange sections	½ cup
Orange juice	½ cup
Papaya	¾ cup
Peach	1 medium
Pear	1 small
Persimmon, native	1 medium
Pineapple	½ cup
Pineapple juice	⅓ cup
Plums	2 medium
Prunes	2 medium
Prune juice	¼ cup
Raisins	2 tablespoons
Tangerine	1 medium
Tangerine juice	½ cup

Note: Cranberries may be used as desired if no sugar is added.

Bread Exchanges

One exchange of bread contains 15 grams of carbohydrate, 2 grams of protein, and 70 calories. Each portion equals 1 exchange.

Bagel, small	½
Barley, cooked	½ cup
Bread:	
Pumpernickel	1 slice (1 oz.)
Raisin	1 slice (1 oz.)
Rye	1 slice (1 oz.)
White (including French and Italian)	1 slice (1 oz.)
Whole wheat	1 slice (1 oz.)
Bread crumbs, dried	3 tablespoons
Cereal:	
Bran flakes	½ cup
Other ready-to-eat, unsweetened	¾ cup
Cooked cereal (see note)	½ cup
Grits, cooked	½ cup
Puffed cereal, unfrosted	1 cup
Wheat germ	¼ cup

Note: The dieter may take liberties when preparing cooked cereal. Weigh the dry cereal to measure ¾ ounce and cook with the amount of liquid directed for one serving. Increase the cooking time to absorb excess liquid and to increase the volume of cereal, or decrease the liquid by 2 tablespoons before adding the cereal. Most uncooked cereals contain 74 calories per ¾-ounce serving.

Cornmeal, dry	2 tablespoons
Crackers:	
Arrowroot	3
Graham (2½-inch square)	2
Matzoh (4 x 6-inch)	½
Oyster	20
Pretzels (3⅛-inch long, ⅛-inch diameter)	25
Rye wafers (2 x 3½-inch)	3
Saltines	6
Soda (2½-inch square)	4
Dinner roll, plain	1
English muffin, small	½
Flour	2½ tablespoons
Frankfurter roll	½
Hamburger bun	½
Legumes: (see note)	
Baked beans (no pork), canned	¼ cup
Beans, peas, lentils (dried or cooked)	½ cup

Note: Dried beans, peas, and lentils may be used as a meat exchange, if desired. One meat exchange equals 2 ounces of cooked, drained legumes.

Pasta, cooked (spaghetti, noodles, macaroni)	½ cup
Popcorn (large kernel), popped with no fat	3 cups
Prepared foods:	
Biscuit, 2-inch diameter (add 1 fat exchange)	1
Corn bread, 2 x 2 x 1-inch (add 1 fat exchange)	1
Corn muffin, 2-inch diameter (add 1 fat exchange)	1
Cracker, round butter type (add 1 fat exchange)	5
Muffin, plain, small (add 1 fat exchange)	1
Pancake, 5-inch diameter (add 1 fat exchange)	1
Potato chips or corn chips (add 2 fat exchanges)	15
Potatoes, French-fried, 2 to 3½ inches long (add 1 fat exchange)	8
Waffle, 5-inch square (add 1 fat exchange)	1
Rice, cooked	½ cup
Tortilla (6-inch diameter)	1
Vegetables:	
Corn	⅓ cup
Corn on the cob	1 small
Lima beans	½ cup
*Parsnips	⅔ cup
*Peas, green (canned or frozen)	½ cup

Potato, white	1 small
Potato, mashed	½ cup
*Pumpkin	¾ cup
*Squash, winter (acorn or butternut)	½ cup
Yam or sweet potato	¼ cup

*See Vegetable Exchanges for dieter's information.

Meat Exchanges (Lean)

Trim off all visible fat. One exchange of lean meat contains 7 grams of protein, 3 grams of fat, and 55 calories. Each portion equals 1 lean meat exchange.

Beans and peas, dried (See dieter's note for Legumes under Bread Exchanges.)	½ cup
Beef:	
Baby beef (very lean), chipped beef, chuck, flank steak, plate ribs, plate skirt steak, round (bottom or top), rump (all cuts), spare ribs, tenderloin, tripe	1 ounce
Cheese:	
Less than 5% butterfat	1 ounce
Cottage cheese, dry or 2% butterfat	1 ounce
Fish (canned):	
Crab, lobster, mackerel, salmon, tuna	¼ cup
Clams, oysters, scallops, shrimp	5 (1 ounce)
Sardines (drained)	3
Fish (fresh or frozen): All kinds	1 ounce
Lamb:	
Leg, loin (roast or chops), ribs, shank, shoulder, sirloin	1 ounce
Pork:	
Leg (whole rump or center shank), ham (smoked or center slices)	1 ounce
Poultry (meat without skin):	
Chicken, Cornish hen, Guinea hen, pheasant, turkey	1 ounce
Veal:	
Cutlets, leg, loin, rib, shank, shoulder	1 ounce

Meat Exchanges (Medium-fat)

Trim off all visible fat. One exchange of medium-fat meat contains 7 grams of protein, 5 grams of fat, and 75 calories. Each portion equals 1 medium-fat meat exchange.

Beef: Corned beef (canned), ground (15% fat), ground round (commercial), rib eye	1 ounce
Cheese:	
Farmer's cheese, Mozzarella, Neufchatel, Parmesan, Ricotta	3 tablespoons
Cottage cheese, creamed	¼ cup

Egg (high cholesterol)	1
Organ meats: (high cholesterol)	
Heart, kidney, liver, sweetbreads	1 ounce
Peanut butter (add 2 fat exchanges)	2 tablespoons
Pork:	
Boiled ham, Boston butt, Canadian bacon, loin (all cuts tenderloin), shoulder arm (picnic), shoulder blade	1 ounce

Meat Exchanges (High-fat)

Trim off all visible fat. One exchange of high-fat meat contains 7 grams of protein, 8 grams of fat, and 100 calories. Each portion equals 1 high-fat meat exchange.

Beef:	
Brisket, corned beef brisket, ground beef (more than 20% fat), ground chuck (commercial), hamburger (commercial), rib roast, steak (club or rib)	1 ounce

Fat Exchanges

One exchange of fat contains 5 grams of fat and 45 calories. One portion equals 1 exchange.

Avocado (4-inch diameter)	⅛
Bacon, crisp	1 strip
Bacon fat	1 teaspoon
Butter	1 teaspoon
Cream, heavy	1 tablespoon
Cream, light	2 tablespoons
Cream, sour	2 tablespoons
Cream cheese	1 tablespoon
Dressings:	
French	1 tablespoon
Italian	1 tablespoon
Salad dressing (mayonnaise type)	2 teaspoons
Lard	1 teaspoon
Margarine (soft, tub, or stick)	1 teaspoon
Mayonnaise:	
imitation	2 teaspoons
regular	1 teaspoon
Nuts:	
Almonds	10 whole
Peanuts	
Spanish	20 whole
Virginia	10 whole
Pecans	2 large, whole
Walnuts	6 small
Other	6 small
Oil (corn, cottonseed, safflower, soy, sunflower)	1 teaspoon
Oil, olive	1 teaspoon
Oil, peanut	1 teaspoon
Olives	5 small
Salt Pork (¾-inch cube)	1 cube

BREADS, CAKES & COOKIES

APRICOT BREAD

Makes 4 servings

12 small *or* 8 medium apricots, fresh (pits removed), canned unsweetened (drained), *or* dried (soaked in ½ cup warm water for 30 minutes)
4 eggs, separated
4 slices whole wheat bread, crumbed
⅔ cup non-fat dry milk
Sweetener to equal ¾ cup sugar
4 teaspoons imitation mayonnaise
1 teaspoon dry natural butter-flavored granules
1 teaspoon baking soda
1 teaspoon almond extract
¼ teaspoon salt
¼ teaspoon cream of tartar

Preheat oven to 350°. In a blender or food processor, combine apricots, egg yolks, bread crumbs, dry milk, sweetener, imitation mayonnaise, dry natural butter-flavored granules, baking soda, almond extract, and salt. In a separate bowl, combine egg whites and cream of tartar; beat until stiff peaks form; fold into apricot mixture. Spray an 8 x 8-inch baking pan with release agent; pour batter into pan. Bake for 50 to 60 minutes, or until toothpick inserted in center comes out clean.

EXCHANGE GUIDE PER SERVING (267 calories)

1 bread
½ milk
1 fruit
1 ounce protein
½ of 1 fat

DELICIOUS BANANA BREAD

Makes 4 servings

4 eggs, separated
¼ teaspoon cream of tartar
4 slices whole wheat bread, crumbed
⅔ cup non-fat dry milk
Sweetener to equal ¼ cup sugar
2 small bananas, sliced
8 teaspoons imitation mayonnaise
4 teaspoons <u>cocoa</u>, optional
1 tablespoon vanilla
1 teaspoon dry natural butter-flavored granules
1 teaspoon baking soda
¼ teaspoon salt

Preheat oven to 350°. In a medium bowl, beat egg whites with cream of tartar until stiff peaks form. In a blender or food processor, combine the remaining ingredients and beat well. Gently fold this mixture into the beaten egg whites. Spray an 8 x 8-inch baking pan with release agent; pour batter into pan. Bake for 35 to 40 minutes, or until toothpick inserted in center comes out clean.

EXCHANGE GUIDE PER SERVING (278 calories)

1 bread
½ milk
1 fruit
1 ounce protein
1 fat
1 Extra

Carrot Cake with Pineapple Cheese Topping, page 13

APPLE AND RAISIN BRAN MUFFINS

Makes 2 servings

⅓ cup (¾ ounce) All-Bran cereal
½ cup buttermilk
¼ cup unsweetened applesauce
1 egg
1 slice bread, torn into pieces
1 teaspoon cinnamon
½ teaspoon baking powder

½ teaspoon vanilla
¼ teaspoon imitation butter-flavored salt
¼ teaspoon baking soda
2 tablespoons raisins, optional
Applesauce Topping (recipe below)

Preheat oven to 350°. Mix cereal, buttermilk, and applesauce; let stand 5 minutes. In a blender or food processor, combine remaining ingredients, except raisins and topping. Blend well; add cereal mixture. Blend; add raisins (if desired). Spoon batter into 6 large or 8 small muffin cups lined with cupcake papers. Bake for 20 to 25 minutes, or until toothpick inserted in center comes out clean. Or, microwave on high setting for 4 to 5 minutes. Meanwhile, prepare Applesauce Topping. Remove from oven; divide Applesauce Topping evenly among muffins.

APPLESAUCE TOPPING

¼ cup part-skim ricotta cheese
¼ cup unsweetened applesauce
1 tablespoon lemon juice

Sweetener to equal 2 teaspoons sugar

Combine all ingredients and mix well. Serve over warm muffins.

EXCHANGE GUIDE PER SERVING (210 calories)
1 bread
1 ounce protein
¼ milk

1½ fruits (if raisins are used)

BREAKFAST SPICE COOKIES

Makes 1 serving

½ medium banana, mashed
⅓ cup instant non-fat dry milk
⅓ cup (¾ ounce) ready-to-eat dry cereal
Sweetener to equal 2 teaspoons sugar
¼ teaspoon baking soda

¼ teaspoon cinnamon
Dash nutmeg
Dash cloves
Dash ginger
⅛ teaspoon imitation butter-flavored salt

Preheat oven to 350°. Mix all ingredients; drop by teaspoonsful onto a cookie sheet that has been sprayed with release agent. Bake for 10 to 15 minutes, or until lightly browned.

EXCHANGE GUIDE PER SERVING (191 calories)
1 bread
1 milk

1 fruit

CARROT CAKE WITH PINEAPPLE CHEESE TOPPING

Makes 4 servings

4 cups grated carrots
4 slices bread, torn into pieces
⅔ cup dry skim milk
  Sweetener to equal ¼ cup sugar
8 teaspoons <u>flour</u>
2 eggs
2 tablespoons imitation mayonnaise
2 teaspoons vanilla

2 teaspoons baking soda
1½ teaspoons cinnamon
1 teaspoon dry natural butter-flavored granules
½ teaspoon nutmeg
¼ teaspoon salt
  Pineapple Cheese Topping (recipe below)

Preheat oven to 350°. In a blender or food processor, combine all ingredients except topping; blend well. Pour batter into an 8 x 8-inch baking pan that has been sprayed with release agent. Bake for 45 minutes, or until toothpick inserted in center comes out clean. While cake is baking, prepare Pineapple Cheese Topping. Cool cake; cover with topping before serving.

PINEAPPLE CHEESE TOPPING

1 cup canned unsweetened crushed pineapple, with juice
½ cup part-skim ricotta cheese

Sweetener to equal 4 teaspoons sugar
1 tablespoon lemon juice

Mix all ingredients well; spread over carrot cake.
Note: This cake may be served warm or cold, but for best flavor, refrigerate overnight before serving.

EXCHANGE GUIDE PER SERVING (342 calories)

1 bread	1 ounce protein
½ milk	¾ fat
½ fruit	2 Extras
2 vegetables	

CHOCOLATE FILLED COOKIE

Makes 1 serving

1 tablespoon imitation margarine
  Sweetener to equal 2 teaspoons sugar
1 teaspoon <u>carob powder</u> *or* <u>cocoa</u>

1 teaspoon shredded <u>coconut</u>
¼ teaspoon vanilla
2 graham cracker squares

Stir together margarine, sweetener, carob, coconut, and vanilla. Spread on a graham cracker; top with remaining cracker.

EXCHANGE GUIDE PER SERVING (128 calories)

1 bread	2 Extras
1½ fats	

LEMON CAKE

Makes 4 servings

½ teaspoon baking soda
1 cup buttermilk
4 eggs, separated
½ teaspoon cream of tartar
Sweetener to equal ½ cup sugar
4 teaspoons imitation mayonnaise

1 teaspoon pure lemon extract
¼ teaspoon imitation butter-flavored salt
Peel of 1 lemon, finely grated
4 slices white bread, torn into pieces

Preheat oven to 350°. Add soda to buttermilk; set aside. In a large bowl, beat egg whites with cream of tartar until stiff peaks form; set aside. In a blender or food processor, beat egg yolks, sweetener, imitation mayonnaise, lemon extract, butter salt, and lemon peel. Add buttermilk mixture and bread pieces; blend well. Fold this mixture in gently with egg whites. Pour into an 8 x 8-inch baking dish that has been sprayed with release agent. Bake for 30 to 35 minutes, or until toothpick inserted in center comes out clean. Serve with a fruit topping, if desired.

EXCHANGE GUIDE PER SERVING (213 calories)

1 bread	1 ounce protein
¼ milk	

PUMPKIN PRUNE BREAD OR MUFFINS

Makes 1 serving

3 medium prunes
¼ cup (¾ ounce) quick-cooking oatmeal
½ cup plus 3 tablespoons canned pumpkin
3 tablespoons non-fat dry milk
1½ tablespoons brown sugar substitute

1 tablespoon flour
1½ teaspoons baking powder
½ teaspoon cinnamon
½ teaspoon vanilla
¼ teaspoon nutmeg
¼ teaspoon maple extract
⅛ teaspoon imitation butter-flavored salt

Preheat oven to 350°. In a small pan, place prunes and cover with water. Bring to a boil; simmer until prunes are puffy. Cool; pit and mash prunes. Mix remaining ingredients, stirring well, and add prunes. Spray a small baking pan or 2 muffin cups with release agent. Pour batter into container. Bake for 30 minutes, or until toothpick inserted in center comes out clean. Or, microwave for 3 to 4 minutes on high setting.

Note: Dieters may count pumpkin as 1 vegetable and omit 1 bread in the serving breakdown.

EXCHANGE GUIDE PER SERVING (232 calories)

2 breads	1½ fruits
½ milk	3 Extras

Lemon Cake with fresh fruit

MICROWAVE CARROT CAKE
Makes 4 servings

4 slices whole wheat bread, torn into pieces
4 eggs, separated
²/₃ cup non-fat dry milk, optional
1½ cups finely grated carrots
Sweetener to equal ¼ cup plus 1½ tablespoons sugar
1 teaspoon dry natural butter-flavored granules
1¼ teaspoons cinnamon
½ teaspoon ginger
½ teaspoon cloves
½ teaspoon baking powder
½ teaspoon baking soda
½ teaspoon salt
1 cup canned unsweetened crushed pineapple, with juice
¼ cup raisins, optional

In a blender or food processor, combine bread, egg yolks, dry milk (if desired), carrots, sweetener, natural butter-flavored granules, spices, baking powder, baking soda, and salt. Blend well. Add pineapple with juice and raisins (if desired); mix. In a medium bowl beat egg whites until stiff peaks form. Fold cake mixture into egg whites; pour into an 8 x 8-inch baking pan that has been sprayed with release agent. Microwave on high for 7 to 9 minutes, or until top springs back when lightly touched.

Note: If milk is omitted, reduce calories by 40 per serving. If raisins are omitted, reduce calories by 62 per serving and consider serving as ½ fruit and no milk.

EXCHANGE GUIDE PER SERVING (250 calories)

1 bread
½ milk
1 fruit
1 ounce protein
²/₃ vegetable

CHOCOLATE COCONUT CAKE
Makes 4 servings

4 slices whole wheat bread, torn into pieces
4 eggs
1 cup sauerkraut, rinsed, drained
²/₃ cup dry skim milk
Sweetener to equal 5 tablespoons sugar
2½ tablespoons cocoa
2 teaspoons coconut extract
1 teaspoon baking soda

Preheat oven to 350°. In a blender or food processor, combine all ingredients; blend well. Pour batter into an 8 x 8-inch baking pan that has been sprayed with release agent. Bake for 35 to 40 minutes, or until toothpick inserted in center comes out clean. Serve with a fruit topping, if desired.

EXCHANGE GUIDE PER SERVING
(210 calories without topping)

1 bread
½ milk
¼ vegetable
1 ounce protein
1 Extra

RICH CHOCOLATE CAKE AND BANANA FREEZE

Makes 4 servings

2 teaspoons baking soda
1 cup sour skim milk *or* buttermilk
4 eggs, separated
¼ teaspoon cream of tartar
4 slices whole wheat bread, crumbed
    Sweetener to equal ½ cup sugar

8 teaspoons cocoa
8 teaspoons imitation mayonnaise
2 teaspoons vanilla
½ teaspoon imitation butter-flavored salt
Banana Freeze (recipe on page 36)

Preheat oven to 350°. Mix baking soda with sour skim milk; set aside. In a medium bowl, beat egg whites with cream of tartar until stiff peaks form. Set aside. In a blender or food processor, combine sour skim milk mixture with egg yolks, bread, sweetener, cocoa, mayonnaise, vanilla, and butter salt. Mix well. Fold into beaten egg whites. Pour into an 8 x 8-inch baking pan that has been sprayed with release agent. Bake 30 to 40 minutes, or until toothpick inserted in center comes out clean. During baking period, prepare Banana Freeze; place in freezer. Serve warm or cold with Banana Freeze or other fruit topping.

EXCHANGE GUIDE PER SERVING (266 calories)

1 bread   1 ounce protein
¼ milk   2 Extras
⅓ fat

MOIST ZUCCHINI CAKE

Makes 4 servings

4 slices whole wheat bread, crumbed
4 eggs
2 cups grated zucchini
1⅓ cups non-fat dry milk
    Sweetener to equal ½ cup sugar
2 tablespoons lemon juice
8 tablespoons flour

1½ teaspoons baking soda
1 teaspoon dry natural butter-flavored granules
1 teaspoon cinnamon
¼ teaspoon nutmeg
⅛ teaspoon cloves
⅛ teaspoon salt

Preheat oven to 350°. In a blender or food processor, combine all ingredients; mix well. Spray an 8 x 8-inch baking dish with release agent; pour in cake mixture. Bake for 40 to 50 minutes, or until toothpick inserted in center comes out clean.

Note: Cake is best served the second day, and it may be served warm or cold.

EXCHANGE GUIDE PER SERVING (312 calories)

1 bread   1 ounce protein
1 milk   2 Extras
1 vegetable

APPLESAUCE OATMEAL COOKIES

Makes 4 servings

2 slices whole wheat bread, torn into pieces
1 cup unsweetened applesauce
½ cup (1½ ounces) quick-cooking oatmeal
2 tablespoons brown sugar substitute

1 tablespoon lemon juice
2 teaspoons dry natural butter-flavored granules
½ teaspoon cinnamon
¼ teaspoon nutmeg
Dash salt
¼ cup raisins

Preheat oven to 400°. In a blender or food processor, mix bread pieces and applesauce. Add remaining ingredients, except raisins. Blend well. Stir in raisins. Spray an 8 x 8-inch baking pan with release agent. Spread mixture in pan. Bake for 30 to 35 minutes, or until golden brown.

EXCHANGE GUIDE PER SERVING (139 calories)

1 bread   1 fruit

NATURAL ORANGE CARROT CAKE

Makes 6 servings

3 cups grated carrots
6 slices whole wheat bread, torn into pieces
1 cup non-fat dry milk
4 eggs plus 2 egg whites; reserve extra yolks
½ cup frozen orange juice concentrate, thawed and undiluted

1 teaspoon baking powder
¼ teaspoon baking soda
⅛ teaspoon salt
1 tablespoon finely grated orange peel
Orange Flavored Topping (recipe below)

Preheat oven to 350°. In a blender or food processor, mix together all ingredients except yolks and topping. Spray a 7½ x 12-inch baking pan with release agent, then pour mixture into pan. Bake for 35 minutes, or until toothpick inserted in center comes out clean. While baking cake, prepare Orange Flavored Topping. When cake is done, spread topping over cake.

ORANGE FLAVORED TOPPING

¼ cup frozen orange juice concentrate, thawed and undiluted
¾ cup water

2 egg yolks
1 tablespoon cornstarch dissolved in 1 tablespoon water

In a small saucepan, combine orange juice concentrate, water, and egg yolks. Heat until thickened. Add cornstarch mixture; continue to cook, stirring constantly, 1 or 2 minutes longer.

EXCHANGE GUIDE PER SERVING (286 calories)

1 bread   1 ounce protein
½ milk   ½ Extra
1 fruit

PIES & FRUIT DESSERTS

ORANGE CREAM PIE

Makes 4 servings

Bread Crust (recipe on page 21)
½ cup frozen orange juice concentrate, thawed and undiluted
2 egg yolks, lightly beaten
2 tablespoons <u>flour</u>
4 teaspoons butter *or* margarine, melted

1 teaspoon dry natural butter-flavored granules
1 cup evaporated skim milk
2 egg whites, beaten until stiff peaks form

Prepare Bread Crust; set aside. Preheat oven to 375°. Mix orange juice concentrate, egg yolks, flour, butter, and natural butter-flavored granules. Add milk, stirring well. Gently fold in beaten egg whites; pour into Bread Crust. Bake pie for 10 minutes. Reduce heat to 350° and bake 50 minutes, or until lightly browned on top.

EXCHANGE GUIDE PER SERVING
(259 calories with Bread Crust)

1 bread	½ ounce protein
¼ milk	1 fat
1 fruit	2½ Extras

CRISPY APPLE-RAISIN DESSERT

Makes 4 servings

½ cup (1½ ounces) Grapenuts cereal
¼ teaspoon cinnamon
⅛ teaspoon nutmeg
⅛ teaspoon cloves
4 teaspoons butter, melted
Sweetener to equal 4 teaspoons sugar, optional
2 small apples, pared and sliced
1 tablespoon raisins

3 tablespoons frozen unsweetened apple juice concentrate, thawed and undiluted
1 teaspoon lemon juice
3 tablespoons water
Dash salt
Pineapple Sherbet, optional (recipe on page 37)

Preheat oven to 350°. Combine cereal, cinnamon, nutmeg, cloves, butter, and sweetener (if desired). Spread over bottom of small baking dish. In a medium bowl, place apples, raisins, juices, water, and salt; toss lightly. Spread evenly over cereal mixture. Cover with foil; bake for 30 minutes, or until apples are fork-tender. Serve warm or cold, plain or topped with Pineapple Sherbet.

EXCHANGE GUIDE PER SERVING
(132 calories without topping)

½ bread	1 fat
1¼ fruits	

BREAD CRUST
Makes 1 crust

4 slices white bread, torn into small pieces

¼ cup water
1 teaspoon vanilla

Preheat oven to 400°. Mix water with vanilla; pour over bread pieces. Stir with a fork; press into an 8-inch pie pan that has been sprayed with release agent. Bake for 10 to 12 minutes, or until golden brown.

EXCHANGE GUIDE PER SERVING (74 calories)
1 bread

CEREAL CRUST
Makes 1 crust

2½ cups (3 ounces) unsweetened flake cereal, crushed
Sweetener to equal 4 teaspoons sugar

¼ cup liquid natural butter-flavored granules

Stir ingredients together; press into an 8- or 9-inch pie pan.

EXCHANGE GUIDE PER SERVING (82 calories)
1 bread

GRAHAM CRACKER CRUST
Makes 1 crust

8 graham crackers (2½-inch squares), crushed
¼ cup butter or margarine, melted

Sweetener to equal 4 teaspoons sugar

Combine ingredients; mix well. Spread on bottom of a 9- or 10-inch pie pan.

EXCHANGE GUIDE PER SERVING (160 calories)
1 bread   3 fats

CANTALOUPE DELIGHT
Makes 4 servings

1 cup plain yogurt
Sweetener to equal 2 teaspoons sugar
½ teaspoon almond extract

2 oranges, sectioned
1 small cantaloupe, cut into bite-sized pieces

Mix yogurt, sweetener, and extract. Blend in fruit; chill before serving.

EXCHANGE GUIDE PER SERVING (88 calories)
¼ milk   1 fruit

LIME PIE WITH CHOCOLATE CRUST

Makes 4 servings

Chocolate Crust (recipe below)
1 cup lemon-lime diet soda
1 package lime-flavored sugar-free gelatin dessert

2 tablespoons lime juice
Sweetener to equal 8 teaspoons sugar
1 cup evaporated skim milk, chilled

Prepare Chocolate Crust; set aside. Bring diet soda to a boil; remove from heat. Add gelatin, lime juice, and sweetener. Stir until gelatin dissolves. Refrigerate until slightly thickened. Beat chilled milk until the mixture has the consistency of whipped cream; fold into partially set gelatin. Pour mixture into Chocolate Crust. Chill until ready to serve.

CHOCOLATE CRUST

3 cups (3 ounces) crisp rice cereal, crushed
8 teaspoons cocoa
Sweetener to equal 8 teaspoons sugar

¼ cup liquid natural butter-flavored granules

Combine cereal and cocoa; add sweetener and natural butter-flavored granules; stir well. Press into an 8- or 9-inch pie pan.

EXCHANGE GUIDE PER SERVING
(142 calories with Chocolate Crust; 98 calories Chocolate Crust alone)
1 bread   2 Extras
¼ milk

RHUBARB STRAWBERRY PIE

Makes 4 servings

1½ cups rhubarb, cut into ½-inch pieces
½ cup strawberry diet soda
1 package strawberry-flavored sugar-free gelatin dessert
Sweetener to equal 4 teaspoons sugar

1 cup evaporated skim milk, chilled
1 prepared pastry shell
Whipped Topping (recipe on page 40)

Combine rhubarb and diet soda; cook until rhubarb is soft. Add gelatin and sweetener; stir until gelatin dissolves. Refrigerate until slightly thickened. Beat chilled milk to the consistency of whipped cream. Fold whipped milk into rhubarb mixture; pour into prepared pastry shell. Refrigerate until set. Top with Whipped Topping.

EXCHANGE GUIDE PER SERVING
(50 calories without crust or topping)
¼ milk   1 vegetable

Lime Pie with Chocolate Crust

PINEAPPLE CHIFFON DESSERT

Makes 4 servings

½ cup lemon-lime diet soda
1 package lime-flavored sugar-free gelatin dessert
  Sweetener to equal 4 teaspoons sugar

2 cups canned unsweetened crushed pineapple, with juice
1 cup evaporated skim milk, chilled
  Graham Cracker Crust, optional (recipe on page 21)

Bring diet soda to a boil; remove from heat. Add lime gelatin and sweetener; stir until gelatin dissolves. Add pineapple; refrigerate until mixture thickens slightly. Beat chilled evaporated milk until the mixture has the consistency of whipped cream. Fold into pineapple mixture. Pour into Graham Cracker Crust or into an 8 x 8-inch pan. Chill until set.

EXCHANGE GUIDE PER SERVING
(186 calories with crust; 89 calories without crust)

1 bread	1 fruit
½ milk	¾ fat

PEACHEESY PIE

Makes 3 servings

Special Bread Crust (recipe below)
3 fresh, frozen *or* canned unsweetened peaches; sliced, drained
¼ cup part-skim ricotta cheese
2 eggs

¾ cup skim milk
  Sweetener to equal ¼ cup sugar
1 teaspoon almond extract
½ teaspoon cinnamon
  Dry sweetener to equal 1 tablespoon sugar

Prepare Special Bread Crust; cool completely. Preheat oven to 350°. Place sliced peaches in wheel spoke design in bottom of baked crust. Combine ricotta cheese, eggs, milk, sweetener, and almond extract; mix well. Pour over peaches. Sprinkle top with cinnamon and dry sweetener; bake 45 to 55 minutes, or until knife inserted in center comes out clean. Chill before serving.

SPECIAL BREAD CRUST

Makes 1 crust

3 slices bread, torn into small pieces
2½ tablespoons water

½ teaspoon vanilla

Preheat oven to 400°. Prepare as directed for Bread Crust (recipe on page 21). Bake 12 to 15 minutes, or until lightly browned.

EXCHANGE GUIDE PER SERVING (237 calories)

1 bread	1 ounce protein
¼ milk	1 fruit

BLUEBERRY CRISP

Makes 4 servings

2 cups fresh *or* frozen blueberries
Sweetener to equal ¼ cup sugar
1⅓ cups cold water
1 teaspoon lemon juice
¼ teaspoon salt
2 tablespoons <u>cornstarch</u> dissolved
in 2 tablespoons water

3½ (3 ounces) large shredded wheat
biscuits, crumbled
¼ cup brown sugar substitute
2 tablespoons margarine, melted
2 tablespoons liquid natural butter-
flavored granules
Whipped Topping, optional

Preheat oven to 350°. In a small saucepan, cook blueberries with sweetener, water, lemon juice, and salt. Stir cornstarch mixture into blueberry mixture. Pour into bottom of an 8 x 8-inch baking pan. Mix biscuit crumbs, brown sugar substitute, margarine, and natural butter-flavored granules. Sprinkle evenly over berry mixture; bake for about 25 minutes, or until mixture is bubbly. Serve plain or with Whipped Topping, if desired.

EXCHANGE GUIDE PER SERVING (185 calories)

1 bread	1½ fats
1 fruit	1½ Extras

PEACH AND RHUBARB CHEESE COBBLER

Makes 2 servings

½ cup sliced unsweetened peaches
1 cup rhubarb, cut into ½-inch pieces
1 cup strawberry diet soda
Sweetener to equal 4 teaspoons
sugar

1 tablespoon liquid natural butter-
flavored granules
¼ teaspoon cinnamon
⅛ teaspoon nutmeg
Cheese Cobbler (recipe below)

Preheat oven to 400°. Place fruit in the bottom of a small baking dish or 2 individual baking dishes. Mix soda with sweetener, natural butter-flavored granules, and spices. Pour over fruit. Spoon Cheese Cobbler evenly over fruit. Bake for 45 minutes or until cobbler is browned.

CHEESE COBBLER

¼ cup part-skim ricotta cheese
1 egg
2 slices bread, torn into pieces
½ teaspoon baking powder

½ teaspoon lemon extract, optional
Sweetener to equal 4 teaspoons
sugar

In a blender or food processor, mix all ingredients. If mixture is too thick to blend easily, add 1 tablespoon of liquid from fruit mixture.

EXCHANGE GUIDE PER SERVING (210 calories)

1 bread	1 ounce protein
½ fruit	1 vegetable

COMPANY FRESH PEACH PIE

Makes 6 servings

Company Pastry Shell (recipe below)
1 6-ounce can frozen orange juice concentrate, thawed and undiluted

¾ **cup water**
⅛ **teaspoon allspice**
2 **tablespoons cornstarch dissolved in ¼ cup water**
6 **peaches, peeled and sliced**

Prepare Company Pastry Shell; set aside to cool. In a small saucepan, combine orange juice concentrate, water, and allspice. Bring to a boil. Add cornstarch mixture; cook and stir until thickened; cool. Place sliced peaches in cooled baked pastry shell; top with glaze. Refrigerate 2 hours before serving.

COMPANY PASTRY SHELL

Makes 1 pastry shell

1 cup flour
½ teaspoon salt

⅓ **cup vegetable shortening**
3 to 4 tablespoons ice water

Preheat oven to 400°. Combine flour and salt. Cut in shortening until particles are about the size of small peas. Gradually add ice water, stirring with fork just until a ball begins to form. Roll out between two sheets of waxed paper. Place pastry in 9-inch pie pan, flute edges, and prick pastry with a fork. Bake for about 10 minutes, or until pie shell is lightly browned.

EXCHANGE GUIDE PER SERVING
(165 calories filling alone; 176 calories pastry alone)

Filling:	Pastry:
1 bread	1 bread
2 fruits	3 fats
1 Extra	

PEACHY BLUEBERRY DESSERT

Makes 4 servings

4 tablespoons plain yogurt
4 peach or pear halves, fresh or canned unsweetened

1 cup fresh or frozen unsweetened blueberries
Sweetener to taste

In each of 4 serving dishes, place 1 tablespoon yogurt; top with peach or pear half. Puree blueberries in a blender; sweeten to taste. Pour ¼ of puree over each serving.

EXCHANGE GUIDE PER SERVING (70 calories)

1/16 milk	1 fruit

Company Fresh Peach Pie

PEACH CRUNCH

Makes 4 servings

4 canned unsweetened peaches, sliced; reserve ½ cup juice from peaches
Sweetener to equal 4 teaspoons sugar
1½ teaspoons cornstarch, optional
¼ teaspoon cinnamon
¼ teaspoon nutmeg
⅔ cup old-fashioned or quick-cooking oatmeal

⅓ cup brown sugar substitute
2 tablespoons margarine, melted
2 tablespoons liquid natural butter-flavored granules
1 tablespoon lemon juice
¼ teaspoon imitation butter-flavored salt

Preheat oven to 375°. Place sliced peaches in an 8 x 8-inch baking dish. Mix sweetener, cornstarch, cinnamon, and nutmeg; toss with peaches. Combine peach juice, oatmeal, brown sugar substitute, margarine, natural butter-flavored granules, lemon juice, and salt. Sprinkle over sliced peaches. Bake for 30 minutes. Serve plain, or with ½ cup skim milk mixed with ¼ teaspoon vanilla.

EXCHANGE GUIDE PER SERVING
(183 calories served plain; 224 calories served with milk)

1 bread	1½ fats
1 fruit	¾ Extra

RASPBERRY BANANA PARFAIT

Makes 4 servings

4 teaspoons cornstarch
Sweetener to equal 2 tablespoons sugar
Dash salt
1½ cups frozen unsweetened raspberries, thawed; reserve juice
2 tablespoons frozen orange juice concentrate, thawed and undiluted

1 teaspoon dry natural butter-flavored granules
1 cup plain yogurt
½ teaspoon vanilla
Sweetener to equal 2 teaspoons sugar
2 medium bananas, sliced

In a small saucepan, combine cornstarch, sweetener, and salt. In a measuring cup, combine reserved raspberry juice and orange juice; add water to make ⅔ cup liquid. Stir into cornstarch mixture; cook and stir until thickened. Add natural butter-flavored granules, stirring well to dissolve. Cool completely. Fold in raspberries. Mix yogurt, vanilla, and remaining sweetener in a small bowl. Slice bananas into this mixture; mix gently. In four parfait glasses, layer raspberry sauce with banana mixture. Chill before serving.

EXCHANGE GUIDE PER SERVING (131 calories)

¼ milk	½ Extra
2 fruits	

PUDDINGS & CUSTARDS

ROYAL PINEAPPLE RICE PUDDING

Makes 2 servings

- 1 cup canned unsweetened crushed pineapple, with juice
- ½ cup diced rhubarb, fresh *or* frozen
- 4 teaspoons brown sugar substitute
- ½ teaspoon rum extract
- 1 cup cooked rice
- 1 cup evaporated skim milk
- ½ cup hot water
- 2 eggs, slightly beaten
  Sweetener to equal 2 teaspoons sugar
- 1 teaspoon vanilla
- ⅛ teaspoon imitation butter-flavored salt
- 1 teaspoon coconut extract
  Nutmeg

Preheat oven to 350°. In a small saucepan, cook pineapple and rhubarb until rhubarb is softened. Add brown sugar substitute and rum extract. Remove ¼ cup of the pineapple mixture; set aside for topping. In a medium bowl, mix together rice, milk, hot water, beaten eggs, sweetener, vanilla, imitation butter-flavored salt, and coconut extract. Add pineapple mixture; pour into a medium baking pan. Sprinkle lightly with nutmeg. Place baking pan in a larger baking pan; add hot water to larger pan to a depth of 1 inch. Bake for 30 to 35 minutes, or until knife inserted in center comes out clean. Serve warm or cold, topped with ¼ cup reserved pineapple topping.

EXCHANGE GUIDE PER SERVING (271 calories)

1 bread	1 ounce protein
1 milk	1 fruit

MOCK TAPIOCA PUDDING

Makes 1 serving

- 1 cup skim milk
- ⅛ teaspoon salt
- 2 tablespoons quick Cream of Wheat cereal
- 1 egg, separated
- 1 teaspoon vanilla
  Sweetener to equal 4 teaspoons sugar
  Fruit sauce, optional

Bring milk and salt to a rapid boil in saucepan or microwave oven. Slowly sprinkle in Cream of Wheat, stirring constantly. Return to a boil, lower heat, and cook until thickened. Beat in egg yolk and vanilla. Cool to room temperature. Beat egg white until stiff peaks form; add sweetener. Fold into cereal mixture. Spoon into a dessert dish; chill until serving time. Serve with a fruit sauce, if desired.

EXCHANGE GUIDE PER SERVING
(243 calories without fruit sauce)

1 bread	1 ounce protein
1 milk	

PUMPKIN CUSTARD

Makes 3 servings

1 package unflavored gelatin
¾ cup evaporated skim milk
2 eggs, separated
2 tablespoons brown sugar substitute

¾ cup canned pumpkin
¼ teaspoon pumpkin pie spice
1 teaspoon vanilla
Pumpkin Custard Topping (recipe below)

Sprinkle gelatin over milk; let soften. In a small saucepan, combine egg yolks and 1 tablespoon of the brown sugar substitute. Bring mixture to a boil, stirring constantly; remove from heat. Add pumpkin and spice. Cool until slightly thickened. Beat egg whites until stiff peaks form; add remaining tablespoon brown sugar substitute. Add vanilla; fold egg whites into pumpkin mixture. Divide custard among 3 dessert dishes; chill in refrigerator until firm. While custard is cooling, prepare Pumpkin Custard Topping. Serve custard with a dollop of topping on each dish.

PUMPKIN CUSTARD TOPPING

¼ cup part-skim ricotta cheese
Sweetener to equal 2 teaspoons sugar

½ teaspoon vanilla

Mix cheese, sweetener, and vanilla; blend well. Divide evenly over Pumpkin Custard.

EXCHANGE GUIDE PER SERVING (117 calories)

½ bread	1 ounce protein
½ milk	

BAKED CUSTARD

Makes 1 serving

1 egg, well beaten
1 cup skim milk
Sweetener to equal 4 teaspoons sugar
½ teaspoon vanilla *or* almond extract

¼ teaspoon dry natural butter-flavored granules
Dash imitation butter-flavored salt
Dash nutmeg

Preheat oven to 325°. Mix all ingredients except nutmeg. Pour into a custard cup; sprinkle with nutmeg. Set cup in baking pan; pour ½ inch hot water into pan. Bake for 1 hour or until knife inserted in center comes out clean. Serve warm or chilled.

EXCHANGE GUIDE PER SERVING (152 calories)

1 milk	1 ounce protein

APPLE PUDDING WITH LEMON SAUCE

Makes 4 servings

4 eggs, well beaten
4 small apples, pared and diced
4 slices dried bread, crumbed
Sweetener to equal ⅔ cup sugar
4 teaspoons baking powder
2 teaspoons almond extract

1 teaspoon cinnamon
1 teaspoon imitation butter-flavored salt
½ teaspoon nutmeg
Lemon Sauce (recipe below)

Preheat oven to 350°. Mix all ingredients; pour into an 8 x 8-inch baking dish that has been sprayed with release agent. Bake for 30 to 35 minutes, or until lightly browned. During baking, prepare Lemon Sauce. Serve with ⅓ cup servings of sauce.

LEMON SAUCE

1⅓ cups lemon-lime diet soda
Sweetener to equal 2 tablespoons sugar
4 teaspoons lemon juice
2 teaspoons grated lemon peel

2 tablespoons liquid natural butter-flavored granules
4 teaspoons cornstarch dissolved in 4 teaspoons cold water

In a small saucepan, combine diet soda, sweetener, lemon juice and peel, and natural butter-flavored granules. Bring to a boil. Stir cornstarch mixture into boiling mixture. Cook and stir until thickened. Makes four ⅓ cup servings.

EXCHANGE GUIDE PER SERVING (235 calories)

1 bread	1 ounce protein
1 fruit	1 Extra

MOCK PUDDING

Makes 1 serving

1 cup skim milk
2 tablespoons (¾ ounce) Cream of Wheat cereal
Dash salt

Sweetener to equal 2 teaspoons sugar or to taste
¼ teaspoon pure lemon extract or ¼ teaspoon maple extract

In a small saucepan, bring milk to a boil; stir in cereal and salt. Cook until thickened. Add sweetener and lemon extract. Serve warm or cold.

VARIATION

Chocolate Mock Pudding:
Add 2 teaspoons cocoa to boiling milk, stirring until well blended. Continue cooking as directed above. Just before serving, stir in ¼ teaspoon vanilla.

EXCHANGE GUIDE PER SERVING
(156 calories if lemon or maple; 171 calories if chocolate)

1 bread	2 Extras
1 milk	

BREAKFAST DUNKIN' LEMON CUSTARD

Makes 2 servings

1 cup skim milk
2 eggs, slightly beaten
    Sweetener to equal 4 teaspoons
    sugar
1 teaspoon dry natural butter-
    flavored granules

1 teaspoon finely grated lemon peel
¼ teaspoon pure lemon extract
    Dash salt
    Dash nutmeg

Preheat oven to 325°. In blender or food processor, combine all ingredients, except nutmeg; mix well. Pour mixture into 2 custard cups; sprinkle with nutmeg. Place custard cups in a baking pan. Add 1 inch of hot water to the pan. Bake for 45 minutes to 1 hour, or until custard is set. Or, microwave at a low or defrost setting for 10 minutes, turning as needed.

Serving Suggestion: While custard is cooling, toast bread and spread with 1 teaspoon butter *or* margarine. Cut toast into four strips; dunk into hot custard.

EXCHANGE GUIDE PER SERVING (172 calories)
1 milk   1 ounce protein

CHOCOLATE PUDDING

Makes 2 servings

2 teaspoons cocoa
4 teaspoons cornstarch
½ cup water
1 cup evaporated skim milk, scalded

Sweetener to equal 4 teaspoons
sugar
1 teaspoon vanilla

Mix cocoa, cornstarch, and water until smooth. Stir cocoa mixture into scalded milk. Cook over low heat, stirring constantly, until mixture thickens. Add sweetener and vanilla, mixing well. Divide into 2 large custard dishes.

EXCHANGE GUIDE PER SERVING (118 calories)
1 milk   3 Extras

CHERRY PUDDING

Makes 2 servings

1 cup plain yogurt
½ cup canned unsweetened crushed
    pineapple, drained
½ cup canned unsweetened *or* fresh
    sour pie cherries

Sweetener to equal 4 teaspoons
sugar
¼ teaspoon almond extract
    Few drops of red food coloring

Mix all ingredients well; divide evenly between 2 dessert dishes.

EXCHANGE GUIDE PER SERVING (89 calories)
½ milk   1 fruit

SHERBETS & ICES

FRUIT ICES

Makes 4 servings

2 cups pureed fresh, frozen, *or*
canned unsweetened fruit
½ cup frozen orange juice
concentrate, thawed and undiluted

2 tablespoons lemon juice, optional
Sweetener to taste

Mix all ingredients well. Freeze in small electric ice cream freezer according to manufacturer's directions or pour into freezer container; freeze until almost set. Remove and beat until smooth. Return to freezer; freeze until firm.

EXCHANGE GUIDE PER SERVING (106 calories)
2 fruits

PEAR WATERMELON SHERBET

Makes 6 servings

1½ teaspoons unflavored gelatin
1 cup skim milk
1 cup evaporated skim milk
2 cups crushed pears (about 6 whole
pears)

Sweetener to equal 2 tablespoons
sugar
1 tablespoon lemon juice
¼ teaspoon watermelon oil *or* extract
4 drops red food coloring

Soften gelatin in ½ cup of the skim milk. Bring remaining ½ cup skim milk to a boil. Pour gelatin-milk mixture into boiling milk; stir to dissolve gelatin. Add evaporated skim milk. Chill until slightly syrupy. In food processor, combine remaining ingredients and milk mixture. Beat until mixture begins to thicken. Pour into an 8 x 8-inch square pan; freeze until firm. Remove from freezer 15 minutes before serving time.

EXCHANGE GUIDE PER SERVING (77 calories)
½ milk   1 fruit

ORANGE GUM DROPS

Makes 6 servings

1 cup boiling water
3 envelopes unflavored gelatin
softened in ½ cup cold water

1 6-ounce can frozen orange juice
concentrate, thawed and undiluted
¼ cup cold water

Add boiling water to softened gelatin; stir until gelatin is dissolved. Add orange juice concentrate and cold water. Pour into an 8 x 8-inch pan; chill until set. Cut into 1-inch squares. Makes about 6 dozen squares.

EXCHANGE GUIDE PER 12 1-INCH SQUARES (70 calories)
1 fruit

Lemon Fruit Ice

STRAWBERRY BANANA SHERBET

Makes 2 servings

1½ cups buttermilk
¾ cup strawberries, crushed
½ banana, mashed

Sweetener to equal 4 teaspoons sugar

Mix all ingredients; freeze in small electric ice cream freezer or pour into freezer container and freeze until partially frozen. Remove from freezer and beat with electric mixer. Return to freezer; freeze until firm.

VARIATIONS

Strawberry Sherbet:
  Increase strawberries to 1½ cups; omit banana.

Banana Sherbet:
  Use one 8-inch banana; omit strawberries.

Peach Sherbet:
  Use 2 medium peaches in place of banana and strawberries.

Banana Blueberry Sherbet:
  Use ½ cup crushed blueberries in place of strawberries.

EXCHANGE GUIDE PER SERVING (115 calories)
1 milk   1 fruit

BANANA FREEZE

Makes 1 serving

½ banana, cut into pieces and frozen
¼ cup evaporated skim milk, chilled
½ teaspoon vanilla

Sweetener to equal 2 teaspoons sugar

In a blender, combine all ingredients; blend until mixture is smooth and thickened, having the consistency of soft ice cream. A few ice cubes may be blended in to thicken the mixture more.

EXCHANGE GUIDE PER SERVING (66 calories)
½ milk   1 fruit

ORANGE GINGER SHERBET

Makes 2 servings

1½ cups fresh buttermilk
4 tablespoons frozen orange juice concentrate, thawed and undiluted

4 teaspoons brown sugar substitute
1½ teaspoons lemon juice
¼ teaspoon ground ginger

Mix all ingredients; freeze in a small electric ice cream freezer or in ice cube trays. If using ice cube trays, partially freeze, beat with electric mixer until smooth, and return to freezer. Freeze until firm.

EXCHANGE GUIDE PER SERVING (128 calories)
1 milk   1 fruit

PINEAPPLE SHERBET

Makes 2 servings

1½ cups buttermilk
1 cup canned unsweetened crushed pineapple, with juice

Sweetener to equal 4 teaspoons sugar

Mix all ingredients; freeze in a small electric ice cream freezer or in ice cube trays. If using ice cube trays, partially freeze, beat with electric mixer until smooth, and return to freezer. Freeze until firm.

EXCHANGE GUIDE PER SERVING (120 calories)
1 milk   1 fruit

CREAMY ORANGE SHERBET

Makes 4 servings

2 cups evaporated skim milk
½ cup frozen orange juice concentrate, thawed and undiluted

2 teaspoons vanilla
Sweetener, optional

Mix all ingredients; freeze in a small electric ice cream freezer or in ice cube trays. If using ice cube trays, partially freeze, beat with electric mixer until smooth, and return to freezer. Freeze until firm.

EXCHANGE GUIDE PER SERVING (136 calories)
1 milk   1 fruit

FROZEN CLOUD

Makes 1 serving

Cereal Crust (recipe on page 21)
¼ cup (¾ ounce) Grapenuts cereal
Sweetener to equal 2 teaspoons sugar
1 tablespoon liquid natural butter-flavored granules
1 fruit serving, frozen, such as ½ banana, ¾ cup strawberries or 2 tablespoons frozen orange juice concentrate, thawed and undiluted

½ cup evaporated skim milk, chilled
Sweetener to equal 2 teaspoons sugar
1 teaspoon extract to complement fruit

Prepare Cereal Crust; set aside. Mix cereal with sweetener and natural butter-flavored granules; place in bottom of medium casserole. In blender, combine frozen fruit, chilled milk, sweetener, and extract. Blend until texture of a milk-shake. Pour into Cereal Crust; freeze 30 minutes. If mixture is frozen solid, leave in refrigerator at least 1 hour to soften before serving.

Note: If extra fats are available, use 1 tablespoon melted butter or margarine in place of liquid natural butter-flavored granules.

EXCHANGE GUIDE PER SERVING (209 calories)
1 bread   1 fruit
1 milk

TOPPINGS & SAUCES

CHOCOLATE SAUCE

Makes 6 servings

1 tablespoon plus 1 teaspoon <u>cocoa</u>
2 tablespoons water
2 teaspoons <u>cornstarch</u>
½ teaspoon dry natural butter-flavored granules

¾ cup evaporated skim milk
Sweetener to equal 6 teaspoons sugar

In small saucepan, combine cocoa, water, cornstarch, and natural butter-flavored granules; stir until well mixed. Add milk; cook, stirring constantly, until mixture comes to a boil. Remove from heat; add sweetener. Cover and chill. Serve over chilled fruit.

EXCHANGE GUIDE PER SERVING (20 calories)
¼ milk   1 Extra

RAISIN SAUCE

Makes 4 servings

4 tablespoons raisins
1⅓ cups water
2 teaspoons lemon juice

4 teaspoons <u>cornstarch</u> dissolved in 2 tablespoons water

In a small saucepan, simmer raisins, water, and lemon juice until raisins are plump. Add the cornstarch mixture; cook until thickened.

EXCHANGE GUIDE PER SERVING (41 calories)
½ fruit   1 Extra

TASTY CHERRY TOPPING

Makes 4 servings

2 cups canned unsweetened pie cherries, drained; reserve juice
1 cup reserved cherry juice (If necessary, add water to complete measure.)
Sweetener to equal 8 teaspoons sugar

1 teaspoon imitation cherry-flavored extract
4 drops red food coloring, optional
4 teaspoons <u>cornstarch</u> dissolved in 4 teaspoons water

In a small saucepan, heat cherries, juice, sweetener, cherry extract, and food coloring (if desired) to a boil. Add cornstarch mixture; cook, stirring until thickened. Serve over Chocolate Coconut Cake or other dessert.

EXCHANGE GUIDE PER SERVING (64 calories)
1 fruit   1 Extra

Fresh fruit with Chocolate Sauce

WHIPPED TOPPING
Makes 8 generous servings

1 envelope unflavored gelatin
softened in ¼ cup cold water
⅓ cup boiling water
1 cup ice water

⅔ cup dry skim milk
Sweetener to equal ¼ cup sugar
1 teaspoon vanilla
1 teaspoon lemon juice

Place large bowl in refrigerator to cool. In a separate bowl, add boiling water to softened gelatin; stir to dissolve. Refrigerate until cool. In chilled bowl, combine ice water, dry milk, sweetener, vanilla, lemon juice, and cooled gelatin mixture. Beat with electric mixer until stiff peaks form, about 5 minutes. Store in air-tight container in refrigerator until ready to serve.
Note: Topping does not keep well overnight because it sets up like gelatin. Cut recipe to meet requirements, or bring to room temperature and whip again.

EXCHANGE GUIDE PER SERVING (11 calories)
¼ milk

FAVORITE FRUIT TOPPING
Makes 1 serving

½ cup favorite canned unsweetened
fruit, with 2 tablespoons juice

Sweetener to equal 2 teaspoons
sugar

Place ingredients in a blender; puree.
Note: For best results with fruits such as peaches, pears, and applesauce, add a dash of cinnamon and nutmeg.

EXCHANGE GUIDE PER SERVING (50 calories)
1 fruit

ALL PURPOSE BAR-B-QUE SAUCE
Makes 3 cups

1 envelope dry natural butter-flavored
granules
1½ cups finely chopped onion
1 clove garlic, crushed
1 16-ounce can tomatoes, finely
chopped; with liquid

1 cup tomato sauce
2 tablespoons tarragon *or* wine
vinegar
2 tablespoons Worcestershire sauce
1 tablespoon brown sugar substitute
1 tablespoon dry mustard

In a medium saucepan, mix all ingredients. Bring to a boil; simmer for 25 minutes, or until onions are translucent. Stir occasionally to prevent sauce from scorching.
Note: Use in place of catsup.

EXCHANGE GUIDE PER SERVING
(32 calories per ¼ cup serving)
1 vegetable *or* 1 Extra

MINT SAUCE

Makes 6 servings

⅔ cup frozen unsweetened apple
  juice concentrate, thawed and
  undiluted
⅔ cup water
4 drops green food coloring

1 drop spearmint oil *or* ¼ teaspoon
  spearmint extract
1 tablespoon <u>cornstarch</u> dissolved in
  1 tablespoon water

In a small saucepan, heat apple juice concentrate, water, food coloring, and spearmint oil. Add cornstarch mixture; cook until thickened. Remove from heat, cool, and store in refrigerator.

EXCHANGE GUIDE PER SERVING (61 calories)
1 fruit   ½ Extra

BLUEBERRY SAUCE

Makes 2 servings

1 cup frozen blueberries, thawed
¼ cup water
½ teaspoon lemon juice
  Sweetener to equal 4 teaspoons
  sugar

¼ teaspoon nutmeg *or* cinnamon
2 teaspoons <u>cornstarch</u> dissolved in
  2 teaspoons water

In a small saucepan, cook blueberries with water, lemon juice, sweetener, and spice. Add cornstarch mixture; cook, stirring until thickened.
Note: Blueberry sauce makes 2 large servings. If desired, use ½ of recipe for tarts; reserve the remaining sauce for pancakes or French toast.

VARIATION

Pineapple-Blueberry Sauce:
  Substitute ½ cup crushed pineapple for ½ cup blueberries.

EXCHANGE GUIDE PER SERVING (54 calories)
1 fruit   1 Extra

HOT STRAWBERRY SAUCE

Makes 4 servings

3 cups fresh *or* frozen strawberries
  Sweetener to equal 3 teaspoons
  sugar

¾ teaspoon vanilla extract
¾ teaspoon brandy flavoring,
  optional

In medium saucepan, heat strawberries and sweetener until bubbly; simmer 10 to 15 minutes. Add extracts; stir well. Serve while sauce is hot, as a topping for cold custard, breakfast cake, etc.

EXCHANGE GUIDE PER SERVING (40 calories)
1 fruit

RAINBOW FRUIT SAUCE FOR HAM

Makes 4 servings

2 cups canned unsweetened fruit cocktail, drained; reserve juice
2 tablespoons brown sugar substitute

1½ tablespoons vinegar
2 teaspoons cornstarch dissolved in
1 tablespoon water

In a medium saucepan, combine reserved juice, brown sugar substitute, and vinegar; bring to a boil. Add cornstarch mixture; cook until thickened. Add fruit cocktail; heat. Serve over ham slices.

EXCHANGE GUIDE PER SERVING (25 calories)
½ fruit   ¼ Extra

SWEET PINEAPPLE CHEESE TOPPING

Makes 1 serving

¼ cup part-skim ricotta cheese
Sweetener to equal 2 teaspoons sugar

¼ cup canned unsweetened crushed pineapple, with juice
1 tablespoon low-calorie apricot jam

Combine all ingredients. Serve on toast.

EXCHANGE GUIDE PER SERVING
(130 calories without toast)
½ fruit   1 ounce protein
1 Extra

YOGURT TOPPING FOR FRESH FRUIT

Makes 2 servings

1 cup plain yogurt
¼ teaspoon nutmeg

Sweetener to equal 4 teaspoons sugar

Mix and chill.
Note: Delicious served over fresh strawberries or fresh pineapple.

EXCHANGE GUIDE PER SERVING (43 calories)
½ milk

APPLESAUCE EXTRA

Makes 1 serving

½ cup unsweetened applesauce
2 tablespoons liquid natural butter-flavored granules
1 tablespoon lemon juice

Sweetener to equal 2 teaspoons sugar
Dash cinnamon
Dash nutmeg

Mix together; serve warm or cold.

EXCHANGE GUIDE PER SERVING (65 calories)
1 fruit

BREAKFAST SPECIALTIES

MOCK EGGS BENEDICT

Makes 4 servings

Benedict Cheese Sauce (recipe below)
4 slices toast
¼ cup liquid natural butter-flavored granules

1 4-ounce can sliced mushrooms, drained; reserve juice
4 poached eggs

Prepare Benedict Cheese Sauce and toast. Set aside. In a small saucepan, heat sliced mushrooms and natural butter-flavored granules. Place toast on serving plates. Top each piece with ¼ of mushrooms, one poached egg, and ¼ of Benedict Cheese Sauce. Serve immediately.

BENEDICT CHEESE SAUCE

1 tablespoon flour
1 tablespoon liquid natural butter-flavored granules
½ cup evaporated skim milk
¼ cup reserved mushroom juice (If necessary, add water to make ¼ cup.)

⅛ teaspoon dry mustard
Dash salt
½ cup (2 ounces) grated Cheddar cheese

In a small pan, combine flour and natural butter-flavored granules; mix well. Gradually add milk, mushroom juice, mustard, and salt. Cook until mixture begins to thicken; then stir in grated cheese. Continue cooking, stirring constantly, until sauce is smooth. Keep warm until ready to serve.

EXCHANGE GUIDE PER SERVING (236 calories)

1 bread	1½ ounces protein
⅛ milk	¾ Extra
fraction vegetable	

APRICOT PINEAPPLE FREEZER JAM

Makes 6 servings

1 pound apricots (weighed with pits)
½ cup canned unsweetened crushed pineapple, with juice

2½ teaspoons orange-flavored sugar-free gelatin dessert

Without peeling, pit and grind apricots. In a medium saucepan, combine all ingredients. Heat just long enough to warm mixture; do *not* boil. Pour into small sterilized bottles or freezer containers. Freeze jam until ready to use.

EXCHANGE GUIDE PER SERVING
(20 Calories per 2½ tablespoon serving)
½ fruit

BREAKFAST BARS

Makes 3 servings

¾ cup quick-cooking oatmeal
¼ cup unsweetened applesauce
4 canned unsweetened apricot
   halves; reserve ¼ cup juice
6 medium dried prunes, pitted and
   chopped
½ cup dry skim milk

2 tablespoons cocoa
2 tablespoons brown sugar substitute
1 tablespoon sesame seeds
¾ teaspoon coconut extract
¼ teaspoon imitation butter-flavored
   salt

Preheat oven to 350°. In a medium mixing bowl, mix all ingredients, including reserved juice, until well blended. Spray an 8 x 8-inch baking pan with release agent; spread mixture in pan. Bake for 15 minutes, or until mixture is not sticky to the touch. Cut into strips while warm.

EXCHANGE GUIDE PER SERVING (188 calories)

1 bread	1 fruit
¼ milk	3 Extras

FAVORITE SNACK

Makes 1 serving

¼ cup unsweetened applesauce
1 tablespoon raisins
   Sweetener to equal 1 teaspoon
   sugar

Dash cinnamon
1 teaspoon lemon juice, optional
1 slice toast

In a small saucepan, simmer applesauce, raisins, sweetener, cinnamon, and lemon juice (if desired) until raisins are plump. Serve over one slice of your favorite toast.

Note: If extra fat groups are allowed, butter the toast before adding the topping.

EXCHANGE GUIDE PER SERVING (132 calories)

1 bread	1 fruit

OATMEAL AND EGG CAKE

Makes 1 serving

½ cup skim milk
¼ cup water
¼ cup quick-cooking oatmeal
¼ teaspoon baking powder

1 egg, slightly beaten
   Sweetener to equal 2 teaspoons
   sugar
½ teaspoon vanilla

In a small saucepan, bring milk and water to a boil. Add oatmeal; cook 1 minute. Cool until lukewarm. Add remaining ingredients; mix well. Cook on a hot griddle sprayed with release agent. Serve warm with fruit topping.

EXCHANGE GUIDE PER SERVING
(208 calories without topping)

1 bread	1 ounce protein
½ milk	

FRENCH TOAST

Makes 1 serving

1 medium egg
Sweetener to equal 2 teaspoons
sugar
Dash cinnamon

Dash salt
¼ teaspoon vanilla
1 slice day-old bread

In a medium mixing bowl, combine egg, sweetener, cinnamon, salt and vanilla; mix well. Dip bread into mixture, turning until most of the mixture is absorbed. Grill in a frying pan sprayed with release agent, pouring the remaining egg mixture on top of the bread. Cook slowly; turn when bottom of bread is golden brown. Serve warm, topped with a fruit topping.

EXCHANGE GUIDE PER SERVING (155 calories)
1 bread   1 ounce protein

ZUCCHINI PANCAKES

Makes 1 serving

½ cup diced zucchini
1 egg
1 slice whole wheat bread, torn
into pieces
3 tablespoons dry skim milk
1 teaspoon flour
Sweetener to equal 2 teaspoons
sugar

½ teaspoon vanilla
½ teaspoon baking powder
⅛ teaspoon baking soda
⅛ teaspoon imitation butter-
flavored salt

Process zucchini and egg in a blender or food processor until smooth. Add remaining ingredients; cook on a hot griddle sprayed with release agent.

EXCHANGE GUIDE PER SERVING (216 calories)
1 bread   1 ounce protein
½ milk   1 Extra
1 vegetable

RED RASPBERRY JAM

Makes 3 servings

8 ounces fresh *or* frozen
unsweetened raspberries (with
juice), crushed

1¼ teaspoons raspberry-flavored
sugar-free gelatin dessert
Sweetener to taste

In a small saucepan, mix crushed berries with gelatin. Heat just long enough to warm mixture; add sweetener to taste. Pour into small sterilized bottles or freezer containers. Freeze all that is not used within a few days.

EXCHANGE GUIDE PER SERVING
(17 calories per 2½ tablespoon serving)
½ fruit

French Toast with Favorite Fruit
Topping, page 40

PUMPKIN PANCAKES

Makes 1 serving

1 slice whole wheat bread, torn into pieces
½ cup canned pumpkin
1 egg
1 teaspoon dry natural butter-flavored granules
½ teaspoon baking powder
⅛ teaspoon baking soda
¼ teaspoon cinnamon
Sweetener to equal 2 teaspoons sugar
Dash salt

Place all ingredients in a blender or food processor; mix well. Cook on a hot griddle sprayed with release agent.
Note: Dieters may count pumpkin as 1 vegetable instead of 1 bread.

EXCHANGE GUIDE PER SERVING (235 calories)
2 bread   1 ounce protein

FRESH FRUIT COMPOTE

Makes 6 servings

2 oranges, peeled, sectioned; reserve juice
1 grapefruit, peeled, sectioned; reserve juice
1 cup cubed cantaloupe
1 medium banana, sliced
¾ cup plain yogurt
¼ teaspoon cinnamon
Sweetener to taste

Prepare fruit over a bowl in order to catch the lost juice. Prepare oranges and grapefruit by paring away the skin and white membrane with a sharp knife and running knife down into sections to lift out the fruit. Mix the yogurt and cinnamon with reserved juice; sweeten to taste. Add prepared fruit; mix well. Divide among six serving dishes. Chill before serving.

EXCHANGE GUIDE PER SERVING (66 calories)
¼ milk   1 fruit

DELICIOUS PRESERVES

Makes 2 servings

1 cup canned unsweetened fruit of choice, such as peaches, pears, apricots, *or* pineapple; reserve ¼ cup juice
2 teaspoons <u>cornstarch</u>
Sweetener to taste
Dash cinnamon *or* nutmeg

Puree fruit. In a small saucepan, mix cornstarch with fruit juice; add pureed fruit and cook until thickened. Add sweetener and spices; serve.
Note: This makes two fruit servings, or enough topping for 4 slices of toast.

EXCHANGE GUIDE PER SERVING (65 calories)
1 fruit   1 Extra

MAIN DISHES

SOY CHICKEN AND MUSHROOMS

Makes 6 servings

⅓ cup soy sauce
½ teaspoon brown sugar substitute
1 teaspoon onion powder
¼ teaspoon oregano
¼ teaspoon rosemary
1 tablespoon wine vinegar
½ tablespoon tarragon vinegar

6 chicken breasts, skinned (average 6 ounces each)
8 ounces fresh mushrooms, sliced
1 tablespoon cornstarch dissolved in 1 tablespoon water
3 cups cooked rice

Preheat oven to 350°. In a small bowl, combine soy sauce, brown sugar substitute, onion powder, seasonings, and vinegars. Place chicken and mushrooms in a 9 x 13-inch pan; pour marinade over. Let stand for 1 hour, turning after 30 minutes. Cover with foil; bake for 45 minutes. Uncover; bake an additional 15 minutes. Remove chicken to a platter; keep warm. Measure drippings; if necessary add enough water to yield 1½ cups. Return drippings to pan. Add cornstarch mixture; cook gently until thickened. Serve chicken and sauce over ½ cup servings of rice.

EXCHANGE GUIDE PER SERVING (306 calories)

1 bread	4 ounces protein
1 vegetable	½ Extra

BEEF BROCCOLI CHOW YUKE

Makes 4 servings

6 dried Chinese mushrooms
2 tablespoons vegetable oil
1 cup thin onion wedges
2 cloves garlic, minced
1¼ pounds flank steak, sliced across grain in 1 x 2¼-inch pieces
¼ teaspoon MSG, optional
Sweetener to equal 1 tablespoon sugar

½ teaspoon salt
1 cup sliced water chestnuts
1 cup sliced bamboo shoots
1 10-ounce package frozen broccoli spears cut into 1½-inch pieces
1½ cups chicken broth
4 teaspoons cornstarch mixed with 2 teaspoons water and ¼ cup soy sauce

Place Chinese mushrooms in enough warm water to cover; soak for 30 minutes. Remove hard stems; cut mushrooms into small wedge-like pieces. In a wok or large skillet, heat oil and sauté onion, garlic, and mushrooms until onion is translucent. Remove vegetables from wok; add meat, MSG, sweetener, and salt. Stir-fry until meat is cooked. Return onion mixture to wok; add sliced water chestnuts, bamboo shoots, and broccoli. Add chicken broth; bring to a boil; cook 3 minutes. Add cornstarch-soy sauce mixture; cook until thickened.

EXCHANGE GUIDE PER SERVING (372 calories)

2½ vegetables	3 ounces protein
1 Extra	

TURKEY AND SAGE DRESSING CASSEROLE
Makes 2 servings

1½ cups (6 ounces) diced cooked turkey *or* chicken
2 slices whole wheat bread, torn into pieces
4 stalks celery, finely chopped
1 tablespoon dehydrated vegetable flakes, optional

2 tablespoons dehydrated onion flakes
1 teaspoon poultry seasoning
½ teaspoon sage
⅛ teaspoon garlic powder *or* to taste
1 teaspoon chicken bouillon granules dissolved in ½ cup hot water

Preheat oven to 350°. In a medium casserole, combine all ingredients, except bouillon mixture. Pour bouillon mixture over meat mixture. Mix well. Bake for 45 minutes to 1 hour.

VARIATION
Mock Turkey Dressing Casserole:
  Substitute 1 6-ounce can of water-packed tuna for turkey; decrease hot water to ¼ cup.

EXCHANGE GUIDE PER SERVING (261 calories)
1 bread   3 ounces protein
1 vegetable

CRAB-STUFFED PRAWNS
Makes 4 servings

12 large prawns, average 1 ounce each
1 cup (3 ounces) fresh mushrooms, diced
3 tablespoons liquid natural butter-flavored granules
1 green onion, minced

2 tablespoons minced fresh parsley
1 teaspoon dry natural butter-flavored granules
1 6-ounce can crabmeat
Dash garlic salt
Lemon juice to taste

Preheat oven to 400°. Devein and butterfly prawns; slash outer edges so that they will lie flat. Place on baking sheet. In a small saucepan, combine mushrooms, liquid natural butter-flavored granules, and onions; sauté. Mix in parsley, dry natural butter-flavored granules, crabmeat, and garlic salt. Divide crab mixture evenly among prawns and sprinkle with lemon juice. Bake until prawns turn pink, about 15 minutes.
Note: If extra fats are allowed, use butter in place of liquid natural butter-flavored granules.

EXCHANGE GUIDE PER SERVING (3 stuffed prawns)
(158 calories with natural butter-flavored granules;
258 calories with butter)
3 ounces protein

VEAL WITH MUSHROOMS

Makes 6 servings

2 pounds boneless veal, sliced ¼-inch thick
Salt and pepper to taste
2 tablespoons butter *or* margarine
½ pound mushrooms, sliced
½ cup chopped onion
1 clove garlic, minced
¾ cup chicken broth

¼ cup white wine
½ teaspoon thyme leaves
1 teaspoon Dijon mustard
¾ cup plain yogurt
2 tablespoons flour
2 tablespoons water
1½ pounds broccoli *or* whole green beans *or* asparagus, cooked

Salt and pepper veal slices. In a large skillet, heat 1 tablespoon butter over medium-high heat. Add veal, a few slices at a time; cook until browned on both sides, about ten minutes. Remove veal; set aside.

In same skillet, heat remaining butter. Add mushrooms, onion, and garlic; sauté until onion is translucent. Add broth, wine, thyme, and mustard; simmer, stirring to loosen browned bits. In a small bowl, mix yogurt, flour, and water until smooth. Stirring vigorously, gradually pour simmering liquid into yogurt mixture; return to skillet. Bring to a boil, stirring constantly for 2 to 3 minutes. Add meat; stir gently until hot. Serve with cooked vegetable.

EXCHANGE GUIDE PER SERVING (375 calories)

⅛ milk
2 vegetables
3 ounces protein
1 Extra

HAWAIIAN MEATBALLS

Makes 4 servings

1½ pounds lean ground beef
2 tablespoons minced green onion
2 tablespoons minced green pepper
½ teaspoon salt
1 tablespoon vegetable oil
1 10¾-ounce can tomato soup

⅓ cup water
½ cup crushed pineapple in unsweetened juice, drained
1 teaspoon soy sauce
Dash ground ginger
2 cups cooked rice, optional

Combine beef, onion, green pepper, and salt; mix well. Shape into 24 meatballs. Heat oil in a large frying pan. Brown meatballs over medium heat; drain fat. Add soup, water, pineapple, soy sauce, and ginger. Cover and cook over low heat for 20 minutes, stirring occasionally. Serve over cooked rice, if desired.

EXCHANGE GUIDE PER SERVING (378 calories without rice; 445 calories with rice)

4½ ounces protein
½ bread (without rice)
¼ fruit
1 fat
1½ bread (with rice)
fraction vegetable

CABBAGE AND TUNA DINNER

Makes 3 servings

1 cup finely chopped onion
4 carrots, sliced
2 cups chicken broth
1 medium head cabbage, shredded
1 teaspoon dry natural butter-
    flavored granules

1 teaspoon salt
1 teaspoon caraway seeds
½ teaspoon paprika
2 6-ounce cans water-packed tuna,
    drained and chunked
2 tablespoons chopped parsley

Place onion, carrots, and 1½ cups chicken broth in a large skillet. Cover and simmer 10 minutes or until vegetables are tender-crisp. Add cabbage, butter-flavored granules, salt, caraway seeds, and paprika. Cook over medium-high heat, stirring frequently, for about 15 minutes or until cabbage is tender-crisp. Add tuna, parsley, and remaining ½ cup chicken broth; mix well. Cook 5 minutes.

EXCHANGE GUIDE PER SERVING (310 calories)

2 vegetables   4 ounces protein

RED SNAPPER ROLLS

Makes 6 servings

1 chicken bouillon cube
1 4-ounce can sliced mushrooms,
    drained; reserve ¼ cup liquid
    (Add water, if necessary, to
    complete measure.)
1 or 2 green onions, chopped
1 clove garlic, crushed
1 10-ounce package frozen chopped
    spinach, cooked and drained
1 teaspoon chicken bouillon granules

1 teaspoon dry natural butter-
    flavored granules
¼ teaspoon nutmeg
    Dash pepper
2 pounds red snapper fillets
1½ tablespoons lime or lemon juice
2 tablespoons butter or margarine
1 tablespoon cornstarch dissolved in
    1 tablespoon water
    Paprika

Preheat oven to 350°. Dissolve bouillon cube in mushroom liquid; add onion and garlic; set aside. Combine spinach, mushrooms, bouillon granules, natural butter-flavored granules, nutmeg, and pepper. Spread mixture on fillets. Roll fish fillets around mixture; secure with toothpicks. Place in a baking pan large enough to hold the fillets in a single layer. Sprinkle with lime juice; pour bouillon mixture over all. Bake uncovered for 30 minutes, or until fish flakes easily with a fork.

Remove fish from baking pan; keep warm. Add butter to drippings; bring to a boil. Add cornstarch mixture to thicken; cook 1 minute. Pour sauce over fish; sprinkle with paprika.

EXCHANGE GUIDE PER SERVING (199 calories)

1 vegetable   3½ ounces protein
1 fat   ½ Extra

TAMALE CHEESE PIE
Makes 4 servings

3 cups (12 ounces) ground turkey
1 cup chopped onion
½ large green pepper, chopped
1 small clove garlic, minced
4 cups whole canned tomatoes with juice

1 to 2 teaspoons chili powder
¾ teaspoon cumin
¾ teaspoon salt
Dash of pepper
Corn Meal Topping

Sauté turkey, onion, green pepper, and garlic in a large skillet. Add tomatoes with juice and seasonings; simmer for 20 minutes. Prepare Corn Meal Topping.

CORN MEAL TOPPING

½ cup corn meal
⅔ cup water
1 teaspoon baking powder

½ teaspoon salt
1 cup (4 ounces) grated Cheddar cheese

Place all ingredients, except cheese, in a medium saucepan; cook over low heat until thickened. Cool slightly; roll to fit an 8 x 8-inch baking dish. Pour turkey mixture into baking dish; cover with Corn Meal Topping. Bake at 375° for 20 minutes. Top with Cheddar cheese; bake an additional 10 minutes.

EXCHANGE GUIDE PER SERVING (335 calories)
2½ vegetables 3 ounces protein
1 bread

SWEET AND SOUR CHICKEN OR PORK
Makes 4 servings

1 green pepper, chunked
2 carrots, cut into 1-inch pieces
1 onion, chunked
1 cup water
1 6-ounce can tomato paste
¼ cup cider vinegar
4 tablespoons frozen orange juice concentrate, thawed and undiluted
2 tablespoons soy sauce
Sweetener to equal 4 teaspoons sugar

⅛ teaspoon garlic powder
½ teaspoon salt
1 cup canned unsweetened chunked pineapple, with juice
1 pound cooked cubed chicken or lean pork
1 tablespoon cornstarch dissolved in 1 tablespoon water

In a large skillet, combine green pepper, carrots, onion, water, tomato paste, vinegar, orange juice concentrate, soy sauce, sweetener, garlic, and salt. Cook until vegetables are tender crisp. Add pineapple and meat cubes; heat well. Add cornstarch mixture; cook until sauce is thickened.

EXCHANGE GUIDE PER SERVING (388 calories)
1 fruit 4 ounces protein
1 vegetable 1 Extra

Sweet and Sour Pork

TASTY BREADED CHICKEN

Makes 6 servings

2½ pounds skinned chicken breasts
   or thighs
1 cup dry bread crumbs
¼ cup low-calorie apricot-pineapple
   preserves
½ cup finely chopped onion
½ cup chicken broth *or* 1 chicken
   bouillon cube dissolved in ½ cup
   hot water

¼ cup cider vinegar
¼ cup soy sauce
1 clove garlic, crushed
1 teaspoon finely grated fresh
   gingerroot

Preheat oven to 350°. Pat chicken dry; place crumbs in a medium-sized bowl. Combine remaining ingredients. Roll chicken in sauce, then in crumbs. Place on baking sheet that has been sprayed with release agent. Bake for 50 to 60 minutes, or until chicken tests fork-tender.

EXCHANGE GUIDE PER SERVING (235 calories)

1 bread	3 ounces protein
¼ vegetable	

MICROWAVE ORANGE CHICKEN

Makes 4 servings

1 3-pound frying chicken, skinned,
   cut into serving pieces
½ cup tomato sauce
½ cup orange juice *or* juice of
   1 orange
¼ cup chopped onion
2 tablespoons soy sauce

Sweetener to equal 2 teaspoons
   sugar
1 teaspoon prepared mustard
½ teaspoon garlic powder
½ teaspoon salt
¼ teaspoon pepper
1 orange, thinly sliced

Place chicken pieces with thick edges outward in a 9 x 13-inch pan. Combine remaining ingredients, except orange slices; spoon over chicken. Microwave on a high setting for 10 minutes; turn chicken; top with orange slices. Continue to cook on high for 8-10 minutes more, or until fork-tender. Let stand 5 minutes before serving.

EXCHANGE GUIDE PER SERVING (309 calories)

½ fruit	4 ounces protein
¼ Extra	

CHICKEN AND BROCCOLI CASSEROLE

Makes 4 servings

1½ cups chicken broth
1 teaspoon chicken bouillon granules
2 teaspoons dry natural butter-flavored granules
1 cup (4 ounces) Velveeta cheese
2 cups (8 ounces) chicken or turkey, diced

2 10-ounce packages frozen broccoli spears, thawed or 1 large bunch broccoli, slightly cooked
24 saltine crackers, crushed

Heat broth, bouillon granules, and butter-flavored granules. Add cheese and stir until melted. Place chicken in a 9 x 13-inch baking dish. Place broccoli on top of chicken, sprinkle with cracker crumbs, and pour cheese sauce over all. Bake uncovered at 350° for 30 minutes.

EXCHANGE GUIDE PER SERVING (324 calories)

2 vegetables 3 ounces protein
1 bread

MEXICAN CABBAGE ROLLS

Makes 4 servings

¾ pound ground turkey
1 cup chopped onion
⅓ cup chopped green pepper
⅓ cup chopped celery
1 clove garlic, chopped
2 cups canned tomatoes
2 cups cooked kidney or pinto beans

1 tablespoon Worcestershire sauce
2 beef bouillon cubes
1 to 2 tablespoons chili powder
1 small head steamed cabbage leaves or 1 medium head cabbage, diced and cooked
¼ cup (2 ounces) Parmesan cheese

Preheat oven to 350°. In a large skillet, sauté turkey, onion, green pepper, celery, and garlic. Add tomatoes, beans, Worcestershire sauce, bouillon cubes, and chili powder; simmer 25 minutes. Meanwhile, steam cabbage leaves or cook diced cabbage. To serve, divide meat mixture evenly among cabbage leaves; roll; place in baking dish. Sprinkle with Parmesan cheese; bake for 15 minutes. If diced cabbage is used, divide meat mixture evenly on beds of cooked cabbage; sprinkle with cheese; bake for 15 minutes.

EXCHANGE GUIDE PER SERVING (340 calories)

1 bread 2½ ounces protein
2 vegetables

VEGETARIAN DISHES

ZUCCHINI PIZZA

Makes 2 servings

1 pound zucchini, sliced in ¾-inch-thick rounds
Pizza Sauce (recipe below)
1 cup (4 ounces) cooked lean ground beef

1 4-ounce can sliced mushrooms, drained
1 medium green pepper, chopped
1 cup (4 ounces) grated mozzarella cheese

Preheat oven to 350°. Spray pizza pan with release agent. Cover the bottom with zucchini rounds. When necessary, cut rounds to fill open spaces. Prepare Pizza Sauce. Pour over zucchini slices. Sprinkle the top with meat, mushrooms, green pepper, and cheese; bake for 45 minutes.

PIZZA SAUCE

1 8-ounce can <u>tomato sauce</u>
1 teaspoon Italian seasoning

½ teaspoon garlic salt
½ teaspoon onion powder

Mix ingredients together; spread over pizza base.

EXCHANGE GUIDE PER SERVING (193 calories)
1 vegetable   2 ounces protein
½ Extra

BARBECUED BAKED BEANS

Makes 4 servings

1 cup canned porkless baked beans

½ cup All-Purpose Bar-B-Que Sauce (recipe on page 40)

Mix ingredients; heat and serve.

EXCHANGE GUIDE PER SERVING (88 calories)
½ vegetable   1 bread

PLAIN SPAGHETTI SAUCE

Makes 2 servings

1 quart <u>tomato juice</u>
½ green pepper, chopped
1 tablespoon onion flakes

½ teaspoon oregano
⅛ teaspoon garlic powder
Salt and pepper to taste

In a heavy skillet, combine ingredients; simmer for 1½ hours. May be used on toast with cheese to make mock pizza.

EXCHANGE GUIDE PER SERVING (109 calories)
2 vegetables *or* 1 Extra

VEGETARIAN SPAGHETTI SAUCE

Makes 4 servings

1 quart tomato juice
2 cups water
1 cup grated zucchini
¼ pound mushrooms, chopped
1 green pepper, chopped
1 clove garlic, crushed

4 teaspoons dried onion flakes
2 beef bouillon cubes
1 teaspoon oregano
1 teaspoon marjoram
1 teaspoon sweet basil
Salt and pepper to taste

Combine all ingredients in a large kettle; simmer about 1½ hours.

EXCHANGE GUIDE PER SERVING (70 calories)
1 vegetable   1 Extra

LOW-CAL VEGETABLE DIP

Makes ½ cup

¼ cup part-skim ricotta cheese
¼ cup plain yogurt
1½ teaspoons dried parsley

¾ teaspoon dill weed
¾ teaspoon dry onion
¾ teaspoon Beau Monde seasoning

Mix all ingredients well; serve with raw vegetables.

EXCHANGE GUIDE PER SERVING
(132 calories per ½ cup serving)
¼ milk   1 ounce protein

CRUSTLESS VEGETABLE QUICHE

Makes 4 servings

1 small zucchini, sliced in ½-inch-
   thick pieces
¼ pound fresh mushrooms, sliced
4 teaspoons butter *or* margarine
1 cup (4 ounces) grated Swiss
   cheese

4 eggs, well beaten
1¾ cups skim milk
2 teaspoons dry natural butter-
   flavored granules
¾ teaspoon salt
Dash white pepper

Preheat oven to 325°. In medium skillet, sauté zucchini and mushrooms in butter until tender crisp. In a 9-inch pie pan sprayed with release agent, place vegetables, then cheese. In a medium bowl, combine eggs, milk, natural butter-flavored granules, salt, and pepper; pour over vegetables. Set pie pan in a larger baking dish; pour hot water into baking dish to a depth of ½ inch. Bake for 1 hour, or until knife inserted in center comes out clean.

EXCHANGE GUIDE PER SERVING (221 calories)
½ milk   2 ounces protein
1 vegetable   1 fat

EGG FOO YUNG CASSEROLE

Makes 3 servings

1 tablespoon liquid natural butter-flavored granules
¼ cup sliced green onion
¼ cup sliced celery
¼ cup chopped green pepper
¼ cup chopped water chestnuts

1 cup bean sprouts, fresh or canned, drained
6 eggs, well beaten
Chinese Brown Sauce (recipe below)

Preheat oven to 350°. In a wok or large skillet, in natural butter-flavored granules, stir-fry green onion, sliced celery, and green pepper until tender crisp. Remove from heat; add other ingredients, except sauce. Pour into a medium casserole that has been sprayed with release agent. Bake about 30 minutes, or until eggs are set. Meanwhile, prepare Chinese Brown Sauce. Spoon Chinese Brown Sauce over each serving.

CHINESE BROWN SAUCE

1 tablespoon liquid natural butter-flavored granules
2 teaspoons cornstarch
Sweetener to equal 1 teaspoon sugar

½ cup water
4 teaspoons soy sauce

In a small saucepan, mix natural butter-flavored granules, cornstarch, and sweetener. Add water and soy sauce; cook until thickened. Keep warm until ready to use.

Note: If fats are not limited, use butter *or* margarine in place of natural butter-flavored granules.

EXCHANGE GUIDE PER SERVING (196 calories)
1 vegetable
1 Extra
2 ounces protein

CHICKEN TERIYAKI

Makes 4 servings

1 medium frying chicken, skinned, cut into serving pieces
½ cup soy sauce
¼ cup dry white wine

1 clove garlic, minced
Sweetener to equal 1 tablespoon sugar

Place chicken pieces in a heavy-duty plastic bag. In a small mixing bowl, combine the remaining ingredients; pour over chicken. Marinate for 1 to 2 hours. During the marinating period, prepare grill, or (about 15 minutes before baking) preheat oven to 350°. On the grill, broil chicken for 12 minutes per side, or until fork-tender. To bake in oven, place chicken pieces in a medium baking dish; bake for 45 minutes to 1 hour, turning pieces after ½ hour.

EXCHANGE GUIDE PER SERVING (216 calories)
3 ounces protein

SALADS
& DRESSINGS

SHRIMP AND MACARONI SALAD

Makes 4 servings

3 cups cooked macaroni
¼ green pepper, minced
3 stalks celery, diced
¼ cup finely chopped onion
2 tablespoons lemon juice
¼ cup plain yogurt
¼ cup Miracle Whip Light

2 tablespoons minced dill pickle
1 tablespoon prepared mustard
  Sweetener to equal 1 teaspoon
  sugar
1 teaspoon salt
6 ounces shrimp, frozen or canned
4 hard-boiled eggs, diced

In a medium bowl, combine macaroni, green pepper, celery, onion, and lemon juice. In a small bowl, blend yogurt, Miracle Whip Light, pickle, mustard, sweetener, and salt. Mix into vegetable-macaroni mixture; add shrimp and eggs. Chill before serving.

EXCHANGE GUIDE PER SERVING (239 calories)

1 bread	3 ounces protein
fraction milk	1½ fats
1 vegetable	

COTTAGE CHEESE AND FRUIT SALAD

Makes 4 servings

1 cup low-fat cottage cheese
1 envelope fruit-flavored sugar-free
  gelatin dessert
  Sweetener to equal 2 teaspoons
  sugar

1 cup canned unsweetened crushed
  pineapple, with juice
  Lettuce leaves

Mix all ingredients; chill. Serve on lettuce leaves.

EXCHANGE GUIDE PER SERVING (78 calories)

½ fruit	1 ounce protein

TOMATO ASPIC SALAD

Makes 4 servings

1 envelope lemon-flavored sugar-free
  gelatin dessert dissolved in ½ cup
  boiling water

1½ cups tomato juice
1 tablespoon red wine vinegar
  Lettuce leaves

In a medium bowl, combine all ingredients except lettuce. Spray 4 small bowls with release agent; divide mixture between bowls and refrigerate until set. Unmold onto lettuce leaves.

EXCHANGE GUIDE PER SERVING (26 calories)
½ vegetable *or* ½ Extra

BREADS, CAKES & COOKIES

Apple and Raisin Bran Muffins, 12
Applesauce Oatmeal Cookies, 18
Apricot Bread, 11
Breakfast Spice Cookies, 12
Carrot Cake with Pineapple Cheese
  Topping, 13
Chocolate Coconut Cake, 16
Chocolate Filled Cookie, 13
Delicious Banana Bread, 11
Lemon Cake, 15
Microwave Carrot Cake, 16
Moist Zucchini Cake, 17
Natural Orange Carrot Cake, 18
Pumpkin Prune Bread or Muffins, 15
Rich Chocolate Cake and Banana
  Freeze, 17

PIES & FRUIT DESSERTS

Blueberry Crisp, 25
Bread Crust, 21
Cantaloupe Delight, 21
Cereal Crust, 21
Chocolate Crust, 22
Company Frest Peach Pie, 27
Company Pastry Shell, 27
Crispy Apple-Raisin Dessert, 20
Graham Cracker Crust, 21
Lime Pie with Chocolate Crust, 22
Orange Cream Pie, 20
Peach and Rhubarb Cheese
  Cobbler, 25
Peach Crunch, 28
Peacheesy Pie, 24
Peachy Blueberry Dessert, 27
Pineapple Chiffon Dessert, 24
Raspberry Banana Parfait, 28
Rhubarb Strawberry Pie, 22
Special Bread Crust, 24

PUDDINGS & CUSTARDS

Apple Pudding with Lemon
  Sauce, 32
Baked Custard, 31
Breakfast Dunkin' Lemon
  Custard, 33
Cherry Pudding, 33

Chocolate Mock Pudding, 32
Chocolate Pudding, 33
Mock Pudding, 32
Mock Tapioca Pudding, 29
Pumpkin Custard, 31
Royal Pineapple Rice Pudding, 29

SHERBETS & ICES

Banana Blueberry Sherbet, 36
Banana Freeze, 36
Banana Sherbet, 36
Creamy Orange Sherbet, 37
Frozen Cloud, 37
Fruit Ices, 34
Orange Ginger Sherbet, 36
Orange Gum Drops, 34
Peach Sherbet, 36
Pear Watermelon Sherbet, 34
Pineapple Sherbet, 37
Strawberry Banana Sherbet, 36
Strawberry Sherbet, 36

TOPPINGS & SAUCES

All-Purpose Bar-B-Que Sauce, 40
Applesauce Extra, 43
Applesauce Topping, 12
Benedict Cheese Sauce, 44
Blueberry Sauce, 41
Chinese Brown Sauce, 61
Chocolate Sauce, 38
Favorite Fruit Topping, 40
Hot Strawberry Sauce, 41
Lemon Sauce, 32
Mint Sauce, 41
Orange Flavored Topping, 18
Pineapple-Blueberry Sauce, 41
Pineapple Cheese Topping, 13
Pizza Sauce, 59
Pumpkin Custard Topping, 31
Rainbow Fruit Sauce for Ham, 43
Raisin Sauce, 38
Sherry Sauce, 73
Sweet Pineapple Cheese
  Topping, 43
Tasty Cherry Topping, 38
Whipped Topping, 40
Yogurt Topping for Fresh Fruit, 43

BREAKFAST SPECIALTIES

Apricot Pineapple Freezer Jam, 44
Breakfast Bars, 45
Delicious Preserves, 48
Favorite Snack, 45
French Toast, 47
Fresh Fruit Compote, 48
Mock Eggs Benedict, 44
Oatmeal and Egg Cake, 45
Pumpkin Pancakes, 48
Red Raspberry Jam, 47
Zucchini Pancakes, 47

MAIN DISHES

Beef Broccoli Chow Yuke, 49
Cabbage and Tuna Dinner, 53
Chicken and Broccoli Casserole, 57
Crab-Stuffed Prawns, 50
Hawaiian Meatballs, 52
Mexican Cabbage Rolls, 57
Microwave Orange Chicken, 56
Mock Turkey Dressing Casserole, 50
Red Snapper Rolls, 53
Soy Chicken and Mushrooms, 49
Sweet and Sour Chicken or Pork, 54
Tamale Cheese Pie, 54
Tasty Breaded Chicken, 56
Turkey and Sage Dressing
  Casserole, 50
Veal with Mushrooms, 52

VEGETARIAN DISHES

Barbecued Baked Beans, 59
Chicken Teriyaki, 61
Corn Pudding, 60
Crustless Vegetable Quiche, 60
Egg Foo Yung Casserole, 61
Plain Spaghetti Sauce, 59
Vegetarian Spaghetti Sauce, 60
Zucchini Pizza, 59

SALADS

Cottage Cheese and Fruit Salad, 63
Shrimp and Macaroni Salad, 63
Tomato Aspic Salad, 63